Spiritual Power and CHURCH GROWTH

C. PETER WAGNER

STRANG COMMUNICATIONS COMPANY
Altamonte Springs, Florida

Creation House
Strang Communications Company
190 N. Westmonte Drive
Altamonte Springs, FL 32714

Previously printed under the title *Look Out! The Pentecostals
Are Coming!*

First printing, June 1986
Second printing, October 1987

Foreword

I met Pete Wagner for the first time approximately 10 years ago. I was attending the Church Growth I course at Fuller Theological Seminary's School of World Mission. Upon entering the classroom that day I encountered a rather warmhearted, disarming man with white hair and a little beard who introduced himself as Pete Wagner.

I had little knowledge of church growth and even less of Peter. And I had no inkling what an important role he would play in my life over the ensuing 10 years. During that first class I came to know Pete as a student and respected and admired him for his intellect and his warm and personable style of teaching. I was amazed at his incredible ability to analyze and organize material in a way that made it easily understood and digestible.

During those two weeks, when I was first exposed to the topic of church growth, God revolutionized my life and gave me a whole new spectrum of study and interest. Church growth is a derivative of the "Third World missionary enterprise," a term coined by Donald McGavran, the founder of the church growth movement. Church growth encompasses several disciplines including theology, anthropology, sociology, some hints of psychology and, most certainly, missiology.

Also, during those two weeks, I became enthralled with the material, as well as the teacher, and became aware that this was going to be a major part of my life's work from that point forward.

A few weeks after the course ended I received a phone call from Pete. He invited me to come and participate in a brand new effort at Fuller Evangelistic Association. FEA was the parent organization Charles E. Fuller developed from which sprang the schools of theology, psychology and ultimately world missions. At that time, Peter was vice president of the organization as well as a professor in the School of World Mission. He asked me to come to FEA and establish a department of church growth. That office began as an extension of FEA's ministry and ultimately became central to all that FEA does. The association has come to be known as the Charles E. Fuller Institute for Evangelism and Church Growth.

During those early days of attempting to develop a consultative arm of ministry to the larger church in the United States and Canada, Pete and I became quite close. I found that he had many admirable qualities, not the least of which was a simple humility and the understanding of who he was and what God had called him to do. Peter is one of the most generous and gentle men I have ever met and at the same time pragmatic to the point of fierceness in defending his evangelical heritage.

Through Pete, I gained insight into the practical application of church growth. He had acquired this knowledge while sitting under Donald McGavran and interacting with the rest of the School of World Mission faculty at Fuller. In those early years at the FEA Department of Church Growth my thinking was molded by Pete and other mentors who were working in the School of World Mission.

One of the chief wellsprings of information was the book you are about to read. In its earliest printing it was labeled *Look Out! The Pentecostals Are Coming*.

Like many conservative evangelical dispensationalists, I took a dim view of anything Pentecostal. Upon reading the book I realized that in spite of what I thought of them at a distance, God was using Pentecostals mightily in South and Central America. This became a major milestone for me because some basic limitations in my education kept me from understanding what God was doing in the world then and today.

This book was originally released in the mid-70s when Pentecostalism was expanding at an unbelievably rapid rate in Asia, Africa, and the South and Central American countries. Groups were evangelizing and growing at a rate only comparable to the first century church. Furthermore, they were demonstrating in their lives that God had not lost His ability to perform signs and wonders and was available and ready to do so with people who would call upon Him to operate in a way He hadn't in the first century.

This was an incredible insight to me, and I recognized that my life was almost devoid of this kind of supernatural phenomena. I was a sincere Christian, prepared in every way I knew to serve God in whatever enterprise He wanted. But now I recognize how very limited

I was in my perception of what it was God wanted to do and could do through me.

This book awakened me to the limitations my theology and training had imposed on my understanding of what God wanted to do in the 20th century. In reading these accounts of Spirit-empowered revival, I realized we, as American evangelicals, were indeed missing something. I sincerely believe that you, the reader, will be deeply challenged by the accounts herein of God's work in Latin America. Peter's historical and statistical research is fascinating. Beginning at the point of the birth of Pentecostalism in Latin America in 1909, he proceeds to trace its development and astounding growth through the ensuing decades.

This is a report not only of facts and figures, but also of personalities, testimonies and heart-rending stories of God's hand upon people today. In this latest edition, Pete further updates the tremendous growth of the church in Latin America. God is continuing to move through the power of His Holy Spirit, utilizing mighty acts to bring people to Himself. This book is essential to the Pentecostal and the non-Pentecostal alike who have sensed in their heart that the evangelical church is missing something.

John Wimber
Vineyard Ministries International
Anaheim, California

Introduction

Never before in human history has a voluntary movement grown as rapidly as Christianity is growing today. Without the aid of political or military forces the message of the kingdom of God is breaking frontiers in vast areas of Asia, Africa and Latin America with extraordinary church growth following.

Within the Christian family the most dramatic expansion is taking place among those called Pentecostals or charismatics. This growth began at the start of the 20th century but did not gain much momentum until after World War II, just before the middle of the century. But as this is being written, only 40 years after rapid growth started, one credible estimate is that there are 160 million Pentecostals/charismatics worldwide. This is not to say that God does not bless non-Pentecostal churches with growth and vitality. He does, and many of them are growing vigorously in many parts of the world. But taken as a group, the growth rate of Pentecostal-type churches is far ahead of any other.

There are places in the world where the most rapidly growing churches would not be listed as Pentecostal, but which exhibit many Pentecostal characteristics such as healing the sick, casting out of demons, miracles and signs. The Lutheran churches of Ethiopia would be an example. In recent years they have been among the fastest growing churches in the world. When a Norwegian Lutheran research team studied the reasons for such phenomenal growth they discovered that, depending on the location, from 60 to 80 percent of the new believers had been drawn to the gospel through firsthand contact with supernatural signs and wonders. Again, the rapidly multiplying churches in China are characterized in every province by miracles, prophecies, deliverances and supernatural manifestations of every kind. Yet the estimated 50 million believers who attend those Chinese churches are not even counted in the 160 million Pentecostals mentioned above.

In the late '60s I became aware of Pentecostal church growth and have been studying it ever since. I wanted to know what God was doing through Pentecostals that caused such dynamic expansion. What was happening there which was not happening in churches that were plateaued, declining or at best growing very slowly? What were we non-Pentecostals missing?

Among Pentecostals, the most rapid growth has taken place in Latin America. I was fortunate enough to have lived in Latin America for 16 years (1956-1971) as a missionary, so I was able to observe Pentecostal church growth there firsthand. I had been trained in church growth research methodology, I was fluent in Spanish and could understand Portuguese, and I had access to the literature in the field as a Latin American scholar. I decided it would make sense to use Latin America as a laboratory. If I could discover the major factors causing church growth among Latin American Pentecostals, I could then derive growth principles which could be of help both to the Pentecostals themselves and to leaders of non-Pentecostal churches.

I myself am not a Pentecostal or a charismatic. As a matter of fact, I should confess that when I first began this research my attitude toward Pentecostals was somewhat less than appreciative and enthusiastic. Later on I will describe some of my anti-Pentecostal behavior in detail.

Suffice it to say that my attitude has changed completely. While not a Pentecostal, I do consider myself a part of the "third wave." I refer to the third wave of the power of the Holy Spirit that has been manifested in the 20th century. The first wave was the Pentecostal movement itself beginning around the turn of the century. The second wave was the charismatic movement beginning in the middle of the century. The third wave, arising in the last quarter of the century, is a manifestation of the same miraculous power of the Holy Spirit in churches and institutions which for various reasons do not wish to be counted as Pentecostal or charismatic.

A major influence causing my own attitude to change was firsthand contact with Pentecostals in Latin America. Once I got to know them I recognized them as brothers and sisters in Christ. I saw God at work among them. I saw exploding churches. I saw preaching so powerful that hardened sinners broke and yielded to Jesus' love. I saw miraculous healings. I saw Christians and their churches multiplying themselves time and again. I saw broken families reunited. I saw the poor and oppressed liberated and restored to dignity through God's living Word. I saw hate turning to love.

All this was impressive. However, I remained a friendly and appreciative spectator until early 1982. Then I became a participant. God used my good friend and colleague, John Wimber, to give me a personal introduction to the realm of the supernatural. It came through a new course which he and I introduced into the Fuller Theological Seminary curriculum called MC510. At the beginning this course was called "Signs, Wonders and Church Growth," and later "Healing Ministries and Church Growth." John taught it for four years. I will never forget my surprise when the Holy Spirit showed up with power right there in the seminary classroom! Week after week I saw miraculous healings, words of knowledge, resting in the Spirit and other visible, tangible manifestations of divine power. I myself was healed, and before I could say "pneumatology" I was a part of it.

Now ministering in the power of the Spirit is characteristic of my regular Christian lifestyle. It is part of my teaching and part of my ministry. In all of my classes prayer is central, and frequently we see remarkable, even miraculous, answers to prayer during the span of a given course. My major ministry outside the seminary is teaching the 120 Fellowship Sunday school class in Lake Avenue Congregational Church. Week in and week out God ministers to us through words of knowledge, healings, deliverances and many gifts of the Spirit. I do not see Fuller Seminary as a charismatic seminary, nor do I see the 120 Fellowship as a charismatic Sunday school class. They are simply part of the third wave. But the work I am now seeing God do through my involvement in the third wave helps me all the more to appreciate and understand what He has been doing for decades in the Pentecostal movement.

That is a major reason for revising this book, originally published in 1973 under the title *Look Out! The Pentecostals Are Coming*. Another reason is that the material needed updating. Pentecostal churches keep growing in Latin America and some of the new material is fascinating. Even if you have read one of the former editions, you will enjoy this because it will bring you up to date.

The book is being used as a text in missions and church growth classes in leading seminaries and Bible colleges. It has been published in Spanish and Portuguese as well as in a British English edition. Pastors and church leaders have found it helpful in understanding the growth dynamics of their own churches. Lay people have read the book and reported that it has drawn them closer to God and caused them to rejoice in His great power. God is speaking through it to Pentecostals and non-Pentecostals alike.

If you feel that in this day of thrilling, unprecedented spiritual harvest there may be something you are missing, my prayer is that the Holy Spirit will use this book to do a new work in your life. I pray that you will know God's power, discover the gifts He has given you, manifest the fruit of the Spirit in your daily life, minister with joy to the body of Christ, draw unbelievers to know the Savior, enjoy a closer intimacy with the Father, and bring glory to God through your life.

C. Peter Wagner
Fuller Theological Seminary
Pasadena, California
January 1986

Chapter One

Pentecostal Growth in Latin America

On the morning of January 14, 1909, a Chilean night watchman had fallen into a deep sleep in his home in Valparaiso. Suddenly Jesus Christ appeared to him in a dream, as clearly as if He had been standing right there in the bedroom. The sleeping man had been a Christian and a member of the local Methodist church for some time, but this had never happened before.

Jesus looked at him and said in a gentle but firm voice, "Wake up. I want to speak to you."

"Yes, Lord!" the startled man replied.

"Go to your pastor and tell him to gather some of the most spiritual people of the congregation. They are to pray together every day. I intend to baptize them with tongues of fire."

Sleep was gone. The man hurried to find his pastor and tell him about the dream—or was it just a dream? For some months, the pastor himself had been

17

anticipating some unusual spiritual blessing. He accepted the dream as a valid revelation from God. The next afternoon a group of dedicated believers met in the parsonage for prayer. They promised each other that they would continue to pray together at 5:00 each afternoon until the Lord fulfilled His promise.

Pentecost in Chile

Extraordinary things began to happen. Believers became deeply concerned for their spiritual lives. Hidden sins were brought to the surface and confessed. Hardened pagans were converted. Several had dreams and visions that confirmed to them that they were on the right road. Great blessing was anticipated and fervently prayed for.

Three months later, by mid-April, the revival had begun. The group in the parsonage in Valparaiso looked upon it as a literal fulfillment of Joel 2:28: "...I will pour out My Spirit on all mankind; and your sons and daughters will prophesy, your old men will dream dreams...." The Spirit was falling in great power.

The Pentecostal movement had come to Chile.

The pastor of that Methodist church was Willis C. Hoover, an American missionary, who had been praying that his church in Chile would somehow see the power of the churches described in the book of Acts.[1] As far back as 1895, Hoover had attended a church in Chicago which was living in a continuing revival, and he was deeply moved. He longed for something similar in his own life. An earthquake had destroyed their church building, and constructing a new one took much time and energy. It was finished in 1908, giving Hoover more time for spiritual things.

Providentially, a tract from India began a slow transformation in his life. One of his wife's schoolmates, who was working among widowed girls with Pandita Ramabai, had sent it. If the Hoovers had not known the author they might not have read it. But it described in detail how the Holy Spirit had fallen with fire among a group of Christians halfway around the world.

Fascinated, the Hoovers began to correspond with other friends in Venezuela, Norway and India, who shared with them their experiences with the Holy Spirit. It was just at this time that the night watchman had his vision, and the afternoon prayer meetings started.

The struggling church began to grow. Sunday school attendance reached 363 in July, 425 in August and 527 in September. Worship services were running between 800 and 900 by October.

In spite of the fact that such church growth had not been seen previously in the Chilean Methodist church, fierce opposition arose against Hoover and the members of his church. The open manifestations of spiritual power were offensive to many. Some local newspaper reports found their way back to the Methodist Missionary Society in New York. One missionary colleague cabled headquarters with the false charge that Hoover had been sentenced by a criminal court in Valparaiso. By the end of 1909 official charges had come against him.

One document accused Hoover of "teaching the doctrines of raising of hands, the baptism of fire, miracles of faith healing, visions, the gift of tongues, prophecies, predicting the date of Christ's return, falling down under the power of the Holy Spirit, and opposition to organized churches." Such things were said to be "anti-biblical and anti-Methodist," and before long the Methodist church had forced Willis Hoover out.

Undaunted, Hoover started separate services and founded the Methodist Pentecostal Church. The growth of this church through the years has been phenomenal. Estimates put its total membership at around 650,000 today.[2] This compares with about 20,000 in the Methodist church which dismissed Hoover.[3]

Hicks' Vision for Argentina

During the same year, 1909, the first Pentecostal missionaries arrived in Argentina. They worked independently at the beginning, but in 1914 they affiliated with the Assemblies of God. Reinforcements were sent from the United States and Canada, and the gospel was proclaimed in Buenos Aires and other places. But in spite of dedication and hard work, over 40 years of ministry had produced only 174 adult church members by 1951.[4]

The Pentecostal missionaries were downhearted. Much of their labor seemed to have been in vain. They prayed for something more. They needed a fresh and unusual outpouring of the Spirit of God. But discouragement grew, for nothing seemed to be happening.

Something was happening, however. In 1952 in Tallahassee, Florida, a 44-year-old evangelist named Tommy Hicks was conducting a series of meetings when God sent him a vision.[5] As he prayed, a map of South America appeared vividly to him. The map was covered with a vast field of yellow grain, bent over and ready for the harvest. As Hicks contemplated the beautiful scene of grain waving under the noonday sun, the stalks of wheat suddenly began to change to human bodies, men and women with their hands raised high. They were crying out, "Come, Brother Hicks, come and help us!"

Hicks interpreted this as a Macedonian vision. From that moment he knew beyond the shadow of a doubt that God had some special task for him in South America. South America? He hardly knew a thing about that part of the world, but there was no mistaking the map he had seen. As he continued to pray, God gave him a prophecy that he wrote in his Bible: "For two snows will not pass over the earth until thou shalt go to this land, for thou shalt not go by boat nor by land but as a bird, flying through the air shalt thou go."

Three months later, in Red Bluff, California, the vision was confirmed. In a pastor's home, after a successful evangelistic crusade, the pastor's wife, while leading in prayer, stretched out her hand toward Hicks and repeated the identical words of his prophecy. He had not mentioned either his vision or his prophecy to anyone, but when he showed the lady what he himself had already written in his Bible, she broke down in tears.

As soon as he could, Tommy Hicks paid all his debts and made arrangements to travel to an unknown land. He had very little money, but suddenly he began to receive an astonishing amount of mail, much of which brought spontaneous contributions. Within 10 days he had enough to purchase a one-way ticket to Buenos Aires, Argentina, with $47 left over. A group of friends saw him off at the Los Angeles International Airport, adding a gift of $200 to his expense money.

"When I stop and think," Hicks now says, "how ridiculous it seemed, that I was going to a land that I did not know and people who did not know me—I could not even speak the language—and had only my ticket and $47. But within my soul I was at peace with God...."[6]

Peron...Peron!

On the last leg of the flight, after some evangelistic meetings in Temuco, Chile, the name "Peron" kept coming to Hicks' mind. He had no idea what "Peron" meant, but he had a strong feeling that God was speaking to him. Hicks called the stewardess and asked, "Do you know anyone around here by the name of Peron?" The stewardess looked rather startled and said, "Yes, Mr. Peron is the president of Argentina."

Hicks' mandate was clear—God wanted him to talk to the president himself.

The missionaries he contacted when he arrived advised him against seeking an interview with the president. In the first place, they doubted whether he would be able to arrange it at all. But then, they feared that if he ever got near the president's office, he would run the risk of being arrested and sent to Tierra del Fuego, Argentina's equivalent to Siberia.

Undaunted, Hicks set out to look for Juan Domingo Peron.

After some persistence, Hicks got into the office of the minister of religion, but that appeared to be as far as he was going. Peron could not handle any more visitors; in fact, the president of Panama was scheduled for an important state visit that day.

Then the minister's secretary came into the office limping. His left leg had turned black and blue, and the muscles had stiffened. The knee was badly swollen, and he asked permission to go home. Hicks suggested they pray about it. The secretary scoffed and said, "If Jesus Christ were here Himself, He couldn't help this leg."

Tommy Hicks walked up to the man, knelt, and put his hands around the ailing knee. He prayed and asked Jesus to show His power. Hicks could feel the muscles begin to loosen. The secretary's eyes widened in astonishment—the pain had disappeared!

Hicks said to the dazed minister, "Can I see the president now?"

"I'll take you myself," he replied with a friendly grin.

God had prepared the way. Juan Domingo Peron was cordial and warm. Toward the end of the interview he embraced Tommy Hicks, thanked him sincerely for his visit, and they prayed together. Peron then instructed his assistant to give Hicks whatever he asked for. The first request made and granted was the use of a large stadium and free access to the government radio and press.

The Great Hicks' Campaign

Studies on the church in Argentina have revealed the crucial importance of the Tommy Hicks' campaign of 1954, not only for the Pentecostals, but also for all other churches which cooperated with the meetings. Arno Enns, who has written the standard church history for Argentina, calls the Hicks' campaign "a sovereign breakthrough by God."[7] The influential book *Latin American Church Growth* says, "Many evangelicals in Argentina, whether or not they agree with Hicks' theology, admit that his meetings broke the back of the rigid Argentine resistance to the evangelical witness."[8]

Hicks preached for 52 days to an aggregate attendance of some two million. A Buenos Aires newspaper reported an attendance of 200,000 at the final meeting. Although other denominations cooperated as well, the services were typically Pentecostal, with divine healing a prominent ingredient. All evangelicals profited, but the Pentecostals particularly began a rapid period of growth which has made them the most numerous group of Protestants in Argentina today.

Brazil, the Giant

During that magic year of 1909, when the revival broke out in Chile and when the first Pentecostal missionaries went to Argentina, God was also working in the lives of an Italian and two Swedes in midwestern United States. He was going to use them to introduce the Pentecostal movement into Latin America's giant nation, Brazil.[9]

Louis Francescon, a humble, unassuming Italian immigrant, had received the baptism in the Holy Spirit and had spoken in tongues at William H. Durham's North Avenue Mission in Chicago in 1907. Moving among fellow Italians, Francescon planted churches (the denomination is now called Christian Church of North America) in California and Pennsylvania.[10] Then in 1909 he found himself under a "strong compulsion" to go to South America, a compulsion which he could explain in no way other than its being the direct leading of God.

It is well-known that large groups of Italians had migrated to Argentina and Brazil, so when Francescon set forth on his first missionary journey (he made 11 in all), he spent a short time among the Italians in Buenos Aires. He then went to Sao Paulo, Brazil.

Sao Paulo had a "little Italy" colony of about 1,300,000 at that time, but Francescon did not know any of them personally. Praying that God would guide him, he sat down to relax on a park bench in one of the city's plazas. There he struck up a conversation with an Italian from the state of Parana and led him to Christ. The man invited him to his home in Plantina, where Francescon was successful in bringing the entire family of seven to Christ. They formed the nucleus of the first Pentecostal church in that area.

Back in Sao Paulo, Francescon made contact with a Presbyterian church in the Bras district. He was invited to preach, which he did in Italian. His message moved many of the church members, and all went well until he brought up the matter of speaking in tongues. Some of the Presbyterians reacted very strongly against this, while others were warmly curious. Tensions developed to the point that the elders ordered Francescon out. He left, but so did several other church members who were attracted by the new Pentecostal emphasis. They were sad, because they felt that God had sent Francescon as a prophet to stir up new life in the Presbyterian church itself. But the Presbyterian leaders would not stand for it, and the split occurred.

This new congregation became the mother church for the *Congregacao Crista no Brasil.* The Bras Presbyterian Church numbers only a few hundred today, while the Pentecostal Church has grown to thousands. As a whole, the *Congregacao Crista* has become one of the largest Protestant denominations in Brazil, with over one million communicant members today. Several of their church buildings seat over 3,000.

The Birth of the Brazilian Assemblies

The largest Protestant denomination in Brazil, estimated at over nine million, is the Assemblies of God. In 1909 two Swedish immigrants to the United States, Gunnar Vingren and Daniel Berg, in an intimate prayer meeting in South Bend, Indiana, received a prophecy telling them to go to Para. Para? They had never heard of a place by that name. So they went to the public library and finally discovered that there was a state in Brazil called Para.

They had no idea as to how they would get to Brazil, but in due time another prophecy came telling them to go to New York and look for a certain man at a certain place. Their available cash was just enough for the night train to New York. They found the man, and he provided them the exact amount of money needed to book third-class passage on a freighter to the city of Belem, capital of Para.

They arrived in 1910, bewildered and exhausted. Their wool suits were hardly appropriate attire for one of the world's hottest tropical cities. They relaxed on a park bench, not knowing what to do next, but praying that God would guide them. He guided them first to a Methodist missionary who introduced them to a friendly Baptist pastor who in turn provided them lodging in some rooms behind the church. All went well until they had learned sufficient Portuguese to begin to preach. Then their Pentecostal tendencies came to the surface, and serious tensions arose in the Baptist church. A small group finally left the Baptist church with Vingren and Berg and formed a new congregation. From it sprouted the Assemblies of God in Brazil.[11] The Belem church itself now counts over 30,000 members, including the circle of its own daughter churches in the immediate area.

The denomination they started now holds the distinction of being the largest Protestant church in all of Latin America.

Dramatic Growth Across the Continent

The growth of the Protestant church in Latin America during the 20th century has been one of the most dramatic episodes in the history of the expansion of the Christian movement. Here is how it is mushrooming:

- In 1900 there were about 50,000 Protestants in Latin America.
- In the 1930s membership passed the 1 million mark.
- In the 1950s it passed the 5 million mark.
- In the 1960s it passed the 10 million mark.
- In the 1970s it passed the 20 million mark.

- By the end of the 1980s it should be around 50 million with 137 million projected by the year 2000.

These figures are heartwarming to say the least. With an annual growth rate of 10 percent or more, the Protestant movement in Latin America is increasing three times faster than the population in general.

Pentecostals are supplying the bulk of this church growth. In 1900 there were no Pentecostals at all in Latin America. By 1950 about 25 percent of Latin America Protestants were Pentecostals. But today estimates run around 75 percent. In other words, three out of every four Protestants in Latin America are Pentecostals. This is what makes Latin America such an excellent laboratory to study the dynamics of Pentecostal church growth.

Chile has the largest proportion of Pentecostals of any Latin American republic with over 90 percent. Little wonder that Chile also has something between 15 and 20 percent evangelicals nationwide, one of the strongest Protestant movements on the continent. The largest evangelical church in Latin America, the Jotabeche Methodist Pentecostal Church, is in Chile, a member of the denomination founded by Willis Hoover.

One third of all Latin Americans live in Brazil, but more like half of the continent's evangelicals are found there. Estimates run up to 20 million evangelicals in Brazil. The Assemblies of God, founded by Gunnar Vingren and Daniel Berg in 1910, has become the largest denomination. By 1980 they had grown to 6 million, then by 1984 they were counting 9 million. During that four-year period they were adding 2,700 members per day! I visited Brazil in 1983 and while in Sao Paulo I attended three churches in three nights. The first one seated 4,000, the second 10,000 and the third 12,000. The latter, the *Deus e Amor* Church, is a renovated factory. All three, as might be expected, are Pentecostal churches.

Churches in Argentina showed a spurt of growth following the Tommy Hicks crusade, but more recently a strong evangelistic movement greater than anything previously seen in that country has centered in the Santa Fe area. Omar Cabrera founded the Vision of the Future movement in 1979, and in five years it had grown to 135,000 believers in 35 different preaching centers. God has given unusually powerful gifts of healing and deliverance to Omar Cabrera and his wife, Marfa, and the subsequent harvest of souls hardly has an equal anywhere in the world.

In past years the gospel spread slowly in Colombia, due largely to 15 years of violent persecution of believers in the 1940s and 1950s. Times change, however, and today Colombia is highly receptive. The Christian Crusade of Colombia, for example, has a church building in Bogota which looks like a warehouse but packs in 2,000 every Sunday. The facility is being expanded to accommodate 8,000. Under the dynamic leadership of its pastor, Marcos Diaz, 120 churches have sprung forth from it directly or indirectly. Some of the daughter churches are running 1,000 in attendance themselves. Exciting worship services, a social ministry which meets the needs of the poor and oppressed, and a regular ministry of healings and miracles continues to draw the unsaved.

Central America, one of the most politically unstable areas of the world, is also one of the global flashpoints of church growth. In El Salvador the Assemblies of God has grown from 20,000 to 80,000 in just five years. Across the board, evangelical churches increased from 250,000 to 750,000 in the 10-year period 1974 to 1984.

Nicaragua's evangelicals were estimated at 3.2 percent of the population in 1979, but by 1983 they were over 12 percent. And this under the Sandinistas, a Marxist government.

Guatemala claims the distinction of the highest percentage of Protestants per capita in Latin America with 25 percent. If the present growth rate continues, within 10 years it will be the first country to have at least half the population evangelical. In one year recently the Assemblies of God in Guatemala grew 44 percent. For the past 11 years the Church of God (Cleveland, Tennessee) has planted on the average of one church in Guatemala every five days, and they have been doing the same in Costa Rica for the past four years. In 1982 the largest known crowd of evangelicals in the history of the Western world, 750,000, gathered together in Guatemala City to hear Luis Palau and celebrate the 100th anniversary of the gospel in Guatemala. That was during the one-year period Guatemala was enjoying the leadership of the continent's first evangelical president, Efrain Rios Montt, himself a Pentecostal from the *Verbo* (Word) Church.

How is all of this happening? What are the secrets of the explosive, sustained growth of the Pentecostal churches in Latin America? What can American Christians and American churches, Pentecostal and non-Pentecostal, learn from our brothers and sisters south of the border? The rest of the book will be an attempt to answer these questions....

Chapter Two

Endued With Power From on High

The first and most essential dynamic underlying Pentecostal growth is the power of the Holy Spirit.

In a sense, of course, this is true of all church growth. The apostle Paul said, "I planted, Apollos watered, but God gave the increase." While God calls His human servants and uses them to carry the gospel to unbelievers, it is only the direct work of the Holy Spirit which can ultimately transfer a person from the power of Satan to the power of God and cause a sinner to be born again.

If such is the case, what is it Pentecostals have but many other sincere Christians seem to be missing?

Willis Hoover, who began the Pentecostal movement in Chile, was a Methodist missionary before becoming a Pentecostal. He was able to see the issue from both sides. Here is the way he explains what he perceives to be the difference:

"I believe that the true secret of this whole thing is

that we really and truly believe in the Holy Spirit—we *really* trust Him—we *really* honor Him—we *really* obey Him—we *really* give Him free rein—we *really* believe that the promise in Acts 1:4-5 and Joel 2:28-29 is for us...."[1]

Hoover underscored all those "reallys" because he deeply felt there was a substantial difference between the way in which the Holy Spirit ministered through him when he was a Methodist and the way in which the same Holy Spirit ministered through him as a Pentecostal. The reason I have quoted Willis Hoover is that his perception seems quite typical of a large majority of others who have spent some time as adult Christian believers outside Pentecostalism and later become Pentecostals. Pentecostals who were born and brought up in Pentecostal homes do not feel this nearly so deeply. Even adults converted in Pentecostal churches do not feel it strongly because they have no previous point of comparison.

I personally can identify with Hoover even though I am not a Pentecostal or a charismatic. I am, however, a participant in the third wave as I explained in the Introduction. I consider 1982 as the year I began participating in the third wave of the power of the Holy Spirit, which means that previous to that I spent 31 years as a born-again Christian at a lower level of spiritual energizing than I have since.

So what happened?

The Four Levels of Faith

As I have wrestled with this question, I have come to see that we as Christians are capable of functioning on four different levels of faith. Moving from one level to another brings us in touch with different degrees of God's power mediated through the Holy Spirit.

The first level of faith is *saving faith*. Paul said to the Philippian jailer, "Believe on the Lord Jesus Christ and you will be saved." This is the door through which people enter into the kingdom of God. It is the level of faith which, by definition, every bona fide Christian has experienced.

The second level of faith is *sanctifying faith*. As we grow in our Christian experience our lives exhibit more and more of the fruit of the Spirit. The characteristics of the fruit of the Spirit are found in Galatians 5:22-23, and one of those is faith. While there are no degrees of saving faith—either you are saved or you are not—there are degrees of sanctifying faith. Some have more sanctifying faith than others. The power which comes through this level of faith is twofold: power to live a godly life and power to witness for Christ.

These two levels of faith were what I had been taught through most of my Christian experience. I knew that God's power saved and sanctified, but not much more. I suspect that Willis Hoover was coming from about the same place when, in 1909, he moved to the fourth level of faith. But before I describe the fourth level, I will mention the third level in passing.

The third level of faith is *possibility-thinking faith*. I get the name from the book *Move Ahead With Possibility Thinking* by my friend, Robert H. Schuller. This is faith for setting bold goals. It is the Hebrews 11:1 faith which is the substance of things hoped for. It is the kind of faith Noah had when he built the ark on dry ground. Not all Christians exercise this kind of faith, I am sorry to report. But those who do find they enjoy a measure of God's power released through them to accomplish things otherwise impossible. I don't want to dwell on this in detail because I want to get to the fourth level which is the most important one for understanding what makes Pentecostals tick.

Fourth-Dimension Faith

The fourth level of faith is *fourth-dimension faith*. Again I took the name from a book title, this time from another pastor friend of mine, Paul Yonggi Cho of the Yoido Full Gospel Church of Seoul, Korea. His book *The Fourth Dimension* influenced me a great deal in this direction. It tells about the kind of faith which releases the power of God for supernatural signs and wonders.

Fourth-dimension faith is what Jesus referred to in Matthew 17:19-20. That was the occasion where the disciples came across a boy with epilepsy caused by a demon. They tried to cast out the demon but could not so they asked Jesus why. He said, "Because of your unbelief." Then he told them that if their faith had been only the size of a mustard seed they could have done it. Jesus, of course, was not referring to saving faith. Nor to sanctifying faith. He was referring to a level of faith that would move mountains, a faith for supernatural miracles.

While not all Pentecostals minister on this fourth level of faith, considerably more of them do than do non-Pentecostals. They actually expect and experience the power of God working through them in healing the sick and casting out of demons on a regular basis as part of the normal Christian experience. This is what Hoover meant when he said, "We *really* give Him free rein."

My earlier Christian teaching not only neglected the fourth level of faith, but it actually opposed it. I was taught that, while the miracles of Jesus and the apostles truly occurred, they stopped with the close of the apostolic age and the completion of the canon of Scripture and that we should not expect them today. Where such miracles seemed to be occurring we were to explain them through ignorance or superstition or psychology or fraud or even satanic counterfeits. For many years this is how I saw Pentecostalism. In my case, making the step to the fourth level of faith took about 15 years. In Willis Hoover's case it was much more rapid.

Baptism in the Spirit and Tongues

How is this step made? Pentecostals explain it as being "baptized in the Holy Spirit." Shortly before Pentecost Jesus told His disciples that in a few days they would be baptized with the Holy Spirit. Then it happened on the day of Pentecost, and the first miraculous activity was communicating the gospel to people from all parts of the Roman Empire in their own dialects. In one day a large number of Jesus' disciples moved to the fourth level of faith, and ministry in the miraculous became characteristic of the spread of the gospel throughout the book of Acts.

This experience has become so normative for Pentecostals that their very name "Pentecostals" has been chosen to identify them with the baptism of the Holy Spirit and speaking in tongues. Some entire Pentecostal denominations guard this distinctive so strictly that they require all their clergy to sign an annual statement asserting that they believe the baptism in the Holy Spirit is a spiritual experience subsequent to salvation and that the initial physical evidence of the baptism is speaking in tongues. In other words, if you have spoken in tongues you know you have been baptized in the Holy Spirit. If you have not spoken in tongues you know that you have not yet been baptized in the Holy Spirit.

Virtually all Pentecostals teach the baptism in the Holy Spirit as a once-for-all experience subsequent to salvation, but not all of them are locked into tongues as the invariable physical sign. The church which Willis Hoover founded, the Methodist Pentecostal Church of Chile, is a case in point.

Instead of speaking in tongues, some Methodist Pentecostals have shown evidence of being baptized in the Holy Spirit by dancing in the Spirit. Others have exhibited uncontrollable joy or increased courage for street preaching or great power in leading others to Christ or healing the sick through prayer or by other signs. Many of them also speak in tongues. But a recent survey indicated that 60 percent of their pastors had never spoken in tongues.[2] Pastor Javier Vasquez of their flagship Jotabeche Methodist Pentecostal Church in Santiago has neither spoken in tongues nor danced in the Spirit. For him the most important gift is the correct interpretation of the Bible.[3]

Regardless of how it is explained theologically and experientially, the end result is that Pentecostals freely operate at the fourth level of faith. One of the reasons why I do not consider myself a Pentecostal or a charismatic is that my understanding of Holy Spirit baptism ties it in with the experience of being born again. If I were to argue the point I would go into 1 Corinthians 12:13 which says, "For by one Spirit we were all baptized into one body." But I don't see any reason for arguing the point. I, along with others in the third wave, join with Pentecostals and charismatics in the fourth level of faith where ministry in the miraculous is a part of everyday Christian lifestyle. This is important. Proving who is right or wrong is not that important.

The Supernatural World View

Those who minister at the fourth level of faith and believe in the day-by-day supernatural operation of the

Holy Spirit in signs and wonders have a distinct advantage in winning the masses of Latin America to faith in Christ. Latin Americans are not nearly as secularized as most North Americans and Europeans. Their world view includes the everyday activity of supernatural forces in normal routines of living. While many North Americans think that stories about demons and angels and evil spirits and witches are mere fairy tales, few Latin Americans would agree.

In Brazil, for example, spiritism permeates the whole culture. Of around 140 million Brazilians, 60 percent are practicing spiritists and a full 90 percent have participated in spiritist activities at one time or another. When the census taker comes, most of these people say they are Catholics, but this is largely a veneer. Brazil is much more of a spiritist country than a Catholic country.

Practicing spiritists serve the devil like practicing Christians serve God. The main reason why people are attracted to spiritism is because of power. The devil has supernatural power to solve human problems. Healings really take place. One spiritist leader, Heber Soares of Manaus, made an agreement with the devil to receive the healing powers of five deceased medical specialists from different parts of the world. He himself subsequently healed 80,000 Brazilians from all kinds of sicknesses, and he never took a cent in payment. His case is well known because a Presbyterian minister, Cayo Fabio, witnessed to him and led him to Christ. The whole story has been written up and published in Portuguese.[4] There is no doubt in either Cayo Fabio's mind or Heber Soares' mind that the power of the supernatural world of evil is real and that the only way to confront this is with the supernatural power of God.

It is also well known that the devil ultimately extracts his payment for his healings and other works. The payment is enslavement and the final destination is hell. The kingdom of Satan has been definitively invaded by the kingdom of God. Jesus defeated the enemy on the cross, but we now live in an age of spiritual warfare until Jesus comes again and Satan's defeat is total. Meanwhile Satan schemes to draw as many away from Christ as he possibly can. He uses people like Heber Soares to solve one problem such as tuberculosis or deafness, only to open them up to two or three more problems which come later and bind them closer to the devil. The work of the devil is a vicious cycle which ends in eternal death.

Christians who operate on the fourth level of faith are in touch with spiritual power which can combat and defeat the activities of Satan head on. Pentecostals have known this all along, and that is one of the key reasons they have been growing so rapidly in Latin America.

Dangers of a Secularized Message

When I was a missionary in Latin America I belonged to a mission agency which was a member of the Interdenominational Foreign Missions Association (IFMA). A part of the membership requirement of IFMA is that all member missions must be non-charismatic. Most of their members interpret this as meaning that they must not become involved in ministries attached to the fourth level of faith. They must not expect miracles and healings and signs and exorcisms and spiritual warfare and prophecies and other Pentecostal types of manifestations to characterize their work on the mission field. I know that this was my own attitude, and as the field director of the mission, I enforced it to the best of my ability.

What I did not realize through those 16 years is that

by doing so, I was communicating a world view that was entirely irrelevant to most Latin Americans I was trying to reach. Oh, I believed in the God up there. But other than saving people and helping them to live a godly life, I did not believe that God had much to do with daily life here on earth. I believed that God had created natural laws and that they were operative. When people got sick it was because of germs or viruses and the cure was a pill or an injection or an operation. When I prayed for the sick I prayed that God's will would be done, as if God sometimes wills people to be sick. Or I would pray that God would give the sick person special patience so they would be able to endure hardship with a good Christian testimony. I did not pray expecting that, in direct answer to my prayer, the person would be healed. As a result none that I know of was healed.

When someone would attribute the cause of illness to evil spirits, I would regard that as superstition and feel sorry for the person. Then I would try to enlighten them so that they could know about germs and viruses and what really caused their maladies. I now realize, to my horror, that I was unwittingly an agent for secularization. My world view derived from the secular humanism which permeates American culture (including our churches and seminaries) and was a much more secular world view than the world view of those I was preaching to, even though I went as a missionary to share what I thought was a spiritual and supernatural message, certainly not a secular message.

No wonder the churches I was working with did not grow that well. An exhaustive research project showed that while our kind of churches throughout Latin America had 42 percent of the missionaries, we had only 5 percent of the evangelical believers. At the same time the Pentecostals had 10 percent of the missionaries and 63 percent of the believers.[5] Back in those days it never occurred to me to ask the question about a possible difference in world view between those of us considered mainline evangelical as over against the Pentecostals.

Power Evangelism

I now see that the Pentecostal approach had a dimension of New Testament evangelism which I was not taught in seminary. Some refer to it as "power evangelism." It is the kind Jesus sent out the twelve to do, saying: "As you go, preach, saying, the kingdom of heaven is at hand. Heal the sick, cleanse the lepers, raise the dead, cast out demons" (Matt. 10:7-8). It was Paul's approach of which he says, "My speech and my preaching were not with persuasive words of human wisdom, but in demonstration of the Spirit and of power" (1 Cor. 2:4). When Paul summed up his style of ministry later on in his career, he said, "For I will not dare to speak of any of those things which Christ has not accomplished through me in word and deed, to make the Gentiles obedient—in mighty signs and wonders, by the power of the Spirit of God" (Rom. 15:18-19).

A part of power evangelism, not too well known as yet, deals with the territorial assignment given by the enemy to high ranking evil spirits in the demonic hierarchy. Certain "powers of the air" (Eph. 6:12) may be in charge of certain geographic regions such as countries, provinces, towns, cities, sections of cities and so forth. One of their responsibilities is to blind the minds of the unbelievers so that the light of the gospel may not shine in (see 2 Cor. 4:4), and they have been successful to one degree or another in many places.

For example, the prevalence of witchcraft throughout

Latin America is surprisingly strong. When sickness or poverty or marital problems or bad luck strike, the first instinct of many Latin Americans is to consult a witch. Curses are common. The occult has a grip on millions. Different kinds of witchcraft appeal to different social levels. The lower class deals with magic and blood sacrifices and fetishes. The middle class is attracted by reading tea leaves and tarot cards. The upper class practices astrology, occult healings and parapsychology. It all comes from the same source.

This power cannot be broken with logical arguments. It can only be broken with greater power. Ralph Mahoney tells the story about a missionary who was distributing literature in a small town on the border of Brazil and Uruguay. The national border ran right along the main street of town. On the Uruguayan side of the street no one would accept the tracts or they would destroy them. On the Brazilian side the people would accept them gladly. As a test he offered tracts to individuals on the Uruguayan side, and again to the same individuals when they crossed the street to the Brazilian side. The same person would refuse on one side of the street and accept with thanks on the other.

Naturally he was curious about this, and he prayed to God for a word. God showed him that on the Brazilian side the "strong man" had been bound, but not on the Uruguayan side. The verse which dealt with this was Mark 3:27: "No man can enter a strong man's house and plunder his goods, unless he first binds the strong man."[6]

Omar Cabrera of Santa Fe, Argentina, is one evangelist who has taken seriously the need to bind the strong man or to break the power of territorial hierarchy. When he goes into a new area he shuts himself up alone in a hotel room over a period of four or five days for intense fasting and prayer. He does battle with the forces of the enemy until he identifies the strong men who have ruled over that territory. Then he wrestles with them and binds them in the name of the Lord. When this happens he just walks into his meeting and announces to the audience that they are free. Sick people begin to get healed and lost people begin to get saved even before he preaches and prays for them.

This kind of power evangelism has caused his movement, Vision of the Future, to grow from 10,000 to 135,000 believers in five years.

Even after three years of personal instruction with Jesus Himself, the disciples needed one more thing before they were to go out on their own—power. Jesus said, "Tarry in the city of Jerusalem until you are endued with power from on high" (Luke 24:49). Although the Pentecostals have known a great deal about that power through the years, they do not have a monopoly on it. It is available to non-Pentecostals as well and, as we have seen, it can become a valuable key to effective evangelism and church growth worldwide.

Chapter Three

Taking the Gospel to the People

If you are thinking of visiting Santiago, Chile, plan your trip over a weekend and spend Sunday afternoon and evening watching the Pentecostals in action. Their open-air meetings have become as much a part of Chilean local color as copper cream pitchers or Araucanian Indian artifacts.

You will have no difficulty in finding the "Canutos," as Chileans have nicknamed their Pentecostals after one of their early leaders. Just take a bus downtown and get off somewhere around the railroad station at about 5:00 in the afternoon. Begin walking in almost any direction, and you will soon see a group of people on a street corner or in a plaza. Chances are they are Methodist Pentecostals from the big mother church called the Jotabeche Church.

As you approach them, you will do well to carry a large Bible. That is like an admission ticket into the circle. If you don't have one, a brother or sister will most likely try to convert you on the spot. You will hear them from a block away singing and reciting Bible verses in unison.

Guitars With Long Red Ribbons

When you get closer, you will see maybe 10 guitars with long red ribbons streaming from them, three or four accordions, and a portable loudspeaker or two. The total group might number anywhere from 30 to a couple of hundred. After hymns and Scripture, one person will take the loudspeaker and begin to preach.

The speaker might be an experienced leader or a recent convert. So deeply do Chilean Pentecostals believe in street meetings that a virtual requirement for a legitimate conversion experience is that you agree to go out on the street the Sunday after your decision and give your testimony as to what God did in your life.

This procedure has two distinct benefits. It first helps the new believers cement their faith in Christ and their relationship to the body. They may be rather inarticulate and scared half to death to speak in public, but this ultimately helps them feel like active participants in the mission of the church in the world. As they speak, their companions are praying them through, making them feel very positive toward the other members of the group.

The second benefit is that, in spite of lack of training and a stuttering delivery, the message preached by the new convert gets through—possibly more than it might for a polished, professional minister. The new believer's testimony carries with it a high degree of credibility, since the speaker can so readily identify with the listeners who come from the same social class, dress the same way, and understand that particular way of speaking Spanish.

When the meeting on one street corner is finished, the spectators are not simply given a piece of Christian literature and invited to come to church "sometime" as they often are by less effective street preachers. Instead, they are urged to "come right along with us to church *tonight.*" Individuals will move out and be sure each spectator is gently persuaded to join the crowd.

For two hours these small groups will slowly move one or two blocks nearer the church and stop for another brief meeting. This continues, meeting after meeting, until they have only enough time to march to the church and arrive at about 6:30, bringing the new visitors with them.

They meet others as they approach the church. More than 1,000 open-air evangelists will have been working in the immediate vicinity of the Jotabeche Church. They fill the streets. Often traffic has to be detoured. The church officers step outside to greet the street-preaching teams as they arrive and file into the sanctuary, singing loudly as they go in.

Does Street Preaching Work?

Many non-Pentecostals think street preaching is old-fashioned. Some regard it as a public spectacle that cheapens the gospel. They may not use these words, but they say, in effect, "Singing and yelling out there on the street are beneath my dignity." Some braver souls may even have tried it on occasion but failed because of inexperience or some other reason. From that they tend to generalize, claiming that "street preaching doesn't work, anyway."

Does it really work? The members of the Jotabeche Methodist Pentecostal Church think it does. If you need proof, they will simply point to their massive sanctuary. The former one, on Jotabeche Street, had a seating capacity of only 5,000, so after many years of overflow crowds standing out in the street, they decided to rebuild. Their new church, on the same block, but facing out on Santiago's main thoroughfare, seats 16,000! Costing over $2 million, it was fully paid for by members' contributions the day it was dedicated in 1974.

Those who analyze what they are doing theologically will tell you they are only obeying Jesus' commands to go and preach the gospel to every creature. But they stress the word *go* in contrast to many others who expect unbelievers to *come*. They are aggressive in their evangelism while slower growing churches are invariably more passive. They untiringly proclaim the message of salvation to the lost, but they are not satisfied with proclamation only. They believe in persuading their unbelieving friends to commit their lives to Christ and become responsible members of His church.

Church-Centered Evangelism

This last phrase, "responsible members of His church," is a key concept in unlocking the secrets of Pentecostal growth. To a very high degree, Pentecostals are church-centered, and this increases their effectiveness.

By "church-centered," I do not mean that they are ingrown and introverted—just the opposite! They know that Christ has commanded them to "make disciples," and they also know that disciples are made from those out there in the world. They do not expect the people to come to the gospel; they diligently take the gospel to the people.

But at that point they do not make the mistake the others who are not so church-centered make. They are not content to see newborn babies left out in the street. They need spiritual care, the milk of the Word (1 Pet. 2:2), which they will not get in the street but in the church. The lambs that are found must be brought into the fold where the shepherds can watch over them, heal their wounds and help them grow. They are not to be left in the ravines where the wild beasts will devour them.

Pentecostals are usually proud of their church. This is why they often seem uninterested in participating in city-wide or nation-wide interdenominational crusades. Their seeming aloofness is not ordinarily due to any lack of love or respect for their brethren in other denominations as much as it is to an intuitive knowledge that the very nature of interdenominational evangelism often separates it too much from the local church.

Incorporation Is a Vital Key

Research shows that evangelistic programs can be attractive, flamboyant, heavily financed, expertly staffed, strongly prayed for but relatively fruitless, if they are not properly related to the local churches as an integral part of the evangelistic program itself.

One of Latin America's top evangelistic preachers once brought this up to me in a personal conversation. He was concerned, he said, as to why his city-wide crusades would produce so many apparent decisions for Christ, but that so little fruit would remain. He was not a Pentecostal, incidentally, although he believed in the baptism in the Spirit and had received it himself. I was equally concerned because one of my students had researched several evangelistic crusades in Cochabamba, Bolivia, where I lived at the time. His report had shown statistically that they had been surprisingly ineffective in "adding to the *church* such as should be saved" (Acts 2:47).

My friend had just held the first of a week-long series of evangelistic meetings in a rented auditorium in

Cochabamba. The building had been filled, and some 50 people had responded to the invitation by coming forward. But he knew and I knew that (apart from some believers in the group who were rededicating their lives to God) very few of those who came forward would be found in the Cochabamba churches six months hence.

He belonged to an evangelistic association which stressed the value of interdenominational crusades. By nature, it was not church-centered. I suggested to him that this might be one of the problems. Holding the meetings in such a non-church building as this rented auditorium did not help the new converts to associate their decision with the local church. Neither did the instruction.

I asked the evangelist, "When you finished leading the people who came forward in the sinner's prayer, what did you counsel them to do next?"

He replied, "Read their Bibles, pray regularly and tell someone else about their decision."

In my opinion there is a mistake here, a mistake that most Pentecostals do not make. There is nothing wrong with Bible reading, praying and witnessing—they are all beautiful Christian virtues. But the evangelist's instructions to the newborn babes left out another Christian virtue that *at that particular moment of their experience* was as important as any of the other three—becoming a committed member of a local body of believers, a church.

This cannot be overstressed. Jesus included "baptizing them" as part of the Great Commission. Baptism in its simplest definition is merely the rite of incorporation into the body of Christ in its local and visible form. When you join a church, you commit yourself not only to God but to other believers. The members of the body encourage and nourish one another. When converts are added to the church, they are likely to go on for Christ.

The Spiritual Delivery Room

One of Buenos Aires' largest and most rapidly growing Pentecostal churches stresses incorporation so much that the pastor was once suspected of holding the doctrine of "baptismal regeneration." Members of his church witness constantly and then bring those who are interested to church on Sunday evening. After the singing, the pastor invites all visitors to stand to receive a gift from the church. The deacons distribute New Testaments to them. He then tells them that, since they came to find out the meaning of the gospel and how to become a Christian, they should not stay in the main sanctuary. "My message will be directed to believers, not to you," he says. He then instructs them to move into another room where some laymen will explain to them how to become Christians.

Once they are in the other room, with some of the church's top personal evangelists, you could correctly predict that the percentage of decisions for Christ is high. But along with this, the percentage of those who become disciples, who are "continually devoting themselves to the apostles' teaching, and to fellowship, to the breaking of bread and to prayer," is high also. Why? Chiefly because they are immediately associated with the church. There is no difference between evangelism and follow-up there.

Three things tie them closely to the church:

1. They make their decision right there in the church. The church, in a sense, is the spiritual delivery room for their new birth. Church members, not a visiting preacher from outside, are the obstetricians.

2. Without apology, they are told that if they are

sincere in committing themselves to Christ, they must immediately obey His command to be baptized. To them, baptism is not something optional that Christians may or may not like to do six months, or two years, or ten years from now. Christ is Lord, and His commandments must be obeyed now. They feel that if an inquirer says, "I want to believe in Christ, but I do not want to follow Him in baptism," there is a real question as to the validity of the decision.

3. The new babes in Christ do not go home alone. A church member is assigned to each one and accompanies him or her to their home. In the usual Latin American fashion, the visitor is often invited into the home and offered a cup of coffee and meets the family. Before leaving, the church member makes arrangements to take the new believer and other family members to church the next Sunday. This helps assure incorporation into the body.

Church-centeredness, then, is important to these Pentecostals in Buenos Aires, just as it is to those in Santiago, Chile. It was also important in a highly significant mass evangelistic crusade in Guayaquil, Ecuador, in 1962.

Two Converts Every Day

Missionaries of the Church of the Foursquare Gospel arrived in Guayaquil in 1957.[1] By 1962 they had a small church of 30 members, hardly growing at all. Billy Graham had recently completed a dramatic crusade in the capital of Quito. Guayaquil, Ecuador's largest city, wanted some of the same. Since Billy Graham himself couldn't come, the churches banded together and held their own crusade. They worked for six months and spent thousands of dollars for a six-day evangelistic campaign in June 1962. The maximum attendance was

6,000, and measurable results were extremely low.

Even though the preacher was not a Pentecostal, the Foursquare Church cooperated with the crusade and suffered disappointment along with the rest. They then began a 24-hour-a-day prayer chain, asking the Lord for something better. The Foursquare people took the initiative for another crusade later that same year, invited a Pentecostal preacher and sought the cooperation of the other denominations. When the time came, however, the other churches refused to cooperate. Some non-Pentecostal leaders even tried to discredit the whole effort and discourage attendance.

The Foursquare brethren were saddened by this turn of events, but they need not have been. It was without a doubt a blessing in disguise, for it forced the crusade to be more church-centered than it might have been if it were interdenominational.

God used many different dynamic forces to bring abundant fruit through this evangelistic effort in Guayaquil. They will be mentioned in due time. But the point we are making here is that when people made their decisions to follow Christ, there was no question at all about church membership—they were expected to become members of the Foursquare Church. Thus, when the crusade was completed after six weeks, a public baptism was held. A remarkable crowd of 30,000 showed up to witness the baptism of 1,500 new converts, all of whom had received instruction and who were willing to commit themselves to the local church as well as to Christ.

For the next four years the momentum continued. An average of 65 new converts were baptized each month for those four years. That is more than two per day. By 1966 the Foursquare had 42 churches with a membership of over 4,000!

How those 42 new churches were established is another story. It will be told in the following chapter.

Chapter Four

Mothers and Daughters

When the Foursquare brethren in Guayaquil, Ecuador, launched the evangelistic crusade described at the end of the last chapter, they were, like many of us, "of little faith." They expected some results, but none would have dared to predict that in a period of six weeks one struggling church of 30 members would become seven churches with 1,500 members.

The Holy Spirit gave them special wisdom, however, when they began to take notice that God was doing something unusual in their midst. Attendance soared from fewer than 1,000 the first night of the crusade to 10,000 the second night, to 20,000 during the second week and to over 30,000 before they had finished. Meetings were held in a large, open field, with listeners standing throughout the two- to three-hour service. When people began to respond to the invitations, committing their lives to Jesus Christ, the brethren in charge immediately began wisely to build "follow-up" right into the crusade.[1]

Training the New Converts

The crusade lasted six weeks, not six days. This extended period of time has proven valuable time and again in concentrated evangelistic efforts in Latin America, although it occurs much too infrequently. But, as the Pentecostals in Ecuador can tell us, it provides opportunity not only to win people to Christ, but also to give them their first spiritual food and help them grow in their tender faith.

As soon as they realized that a substantial number of people had been converted, the leaders changed the order of service of the crusade meetings. For one-half hour before the evangelistic service started, they offered a class of basic Bible instruction for new believers. The evangelist's wife took charge of this, and by the time the six weeks were over the converts were well aware of what the Christian life was all about. Of those, 1,500 were ready for baptism.

But what do you do with 1,500 baptized Christians? The Foursquare Church sanctuary couldn't hold a fraction of them. Furthermore, they came from all over Guayaquil, and travel would be a problem in getting them together regularly. The inescapable conclusion was that several different churches had to be started around the city.

Instant Pastors

This was a problem, especially since it hadn't been anticipated. No careful, strategic plans had been laid. But the Foursquare missionary, Roberto Aguirre, was courageous enough to do just about the only thing he could do. He called together the Sunday school teachers, a typical group of busy lay Christians who were struggling with the burden of making a living for their families but desirous of serving God in some way. Aguirre described the problem to them. He suggested that the only way to care for the new believers was to start more churches. The Sunday school teachers agreed with him.

Then he tossed out the bomb. "You people," he said, "are going to be the pastors!"

Eyes widened and mouths dropped. It was one thing to teach Bible for an hour on Sunday morning to a small group of eighth graders. It was something far different to be responsible for a sizable church in the city of Guayaquil. But as they prayed together, their faith grew and they trusted God for whatever was necessary to care for the new believers and continue their efforts to win not only Guayaquil, but all of Ecuador, for Christ.

Seven new churches began immediately. The young believers not only received spiritual food and straightened out their lives, but they began to win other friends and neighbors. One of the interesting sidelights of the whole movement occurred, of all places, in the city marriage license bureau. The officials were so flooded with men and women desirous of straightening out their twisted family situations that they completely ran out of printed marriage license forms and had to close the office until new ones were printed!

Through a combination of the force of circumstances and direction that could only have come from God Himself, the Foursquare Church in Guayaquil learned a lesson that careful research has proved to be valid, not only in Latin America, but in almost any part of the world. Church growth is usually rapid where not only individuals are being won to Christ, but where simultaneously *churches are being multiplied*. This was continued in Ecuador, so that in four years the one church in Guayaquil had become 42 churches all over the republic.

Planting Churches in Colombia

It also happened in Colombia. The rapidly growing United Pentecostal Church has risen to first place numerically among Colombia's Protestant churches largely on this principle. According to Donald Palmer, who has written a full survey of Colombian Pentecostal churches, this is an established pattern.[2] Churches which are growing rapidly in Colombia are precisely those which are actively multiplying local congregations. Between 1960 and 1970, the Assemblies of God planted 50 new churches, the Pan-American Mission 36 new churches, the Foursquare 45, and the United Pentecostal an incredible 357. These four healthy denominations are all Pentecostal, and they all practice the principle of church multiplication.

In contrast, the Cumberland Presbyterian Church, which has been in Colombia longer than any of the Pentecostal churches, is one of Colombia's slowest growing churches. In that same 10-year period (1960-1970) they planted only one new church. Not only in Colombia, but in most places in the world, there is a direct correlation between new congregational starts and the rate of church growth. Here the growth of Cumberland Presbyterians at 44 percent per decade contrasts to Pentecostal growth at over 500 percent per decade.[3] Time and again research has confirmed that planting new churches is the most effective evangelistic methodology known under heaven.

A Mile and a Half of Pews

A dramatic illustration of Pentecostal church reproduction is found in the Brazil for Christ Church in Sao

Paulo, Brazil.[4] This is the church led by Manoel de Melo, one of the best known Pentecostal leaders not only in Latin America but in the world.

Under de Melo's leadership the Brazil for Christ Church constructed an awesome 35,000-square-foot sanctuary in downtown Sao Paulo. It seats 10,000 comfortably, but crowds of upwards of 25,000 have been reported for special events. I recall a visit several years ago when the sanctuary was only partially constructed. The meetings were held in the narthex which was said to seat 5,000. I looked over the vast meeting hall and said, "How many pews are in here?" The man showing us around said, "I don't know—we ordered a mile and a half!"

Unless you know the system beforehand, even more surprising than the huge building is the size of the congregation that meets on Sunday morning. It numbers perhaps 100! You immediately ask, "Where are the thousands?"

The thousands meet on Saturday night, but on Sunday they are out where active Christians are supposed to be, according to Manoel de Melo. They are back in their neighborhoods winning new people to Christ and gathering them together in daughter churches. The big building is the mother, an active reproducer. In fact, she might hold the world's record for spiritual offspring. In the city of Sao Paulo alone 1,000 new churches and congregations have been planted by enthusiastic members of the Brazil for Christ Church.

Statistics are not easy to keep up with in such a skyrocketing movement, but according to a careful estimate, Brazil for Christ nationwide has about 6,000 organized churches with 1.2 million members.[5]

Born into a poor family in northeast Brazil, Manoel

de Melo was one of 24 children, all from the same mother. His mother contracted stomach cancer when she was four months pregnant with Manoel, and an abortion was recommended. She went into a cotton field and poured out her heart to God. God said, "The baby you are carrying is going to be born." Her cancer was healed at six months of pregnancy. When Manoel was born his mother placed a Bible on him and consecrated him to the Lord. Knowing that he had been chosen from his mother's womb, Manoel was sensitive to the presence of God. At age seven he received a prophecy which said, "You are going to build a huge temple for Me in Sao Paulo." This was his call to the ministry.

He went to Sao Paulo, married, joined an Assemblies of God church and became a successful architect. He built 150 buildings in Sao Paulo and made a large amount of money. But when he was 25 years of age, driving in his Jeep, he heard God's voice say, "Stop everything. Sell your business and dedicate your life totally to Me." His wife and family were shocked when he told them, so he kept working. Two weeks later on a busy downhill street in Sao Paulo his brakes went completely out. He raced at 60 miles per hour through heavy traffic, then up a hill and stopped without hitting anyone. God's voice came again, "This is the first warning. If you don't obey Me, the next time you will die!"

Needless to say, Manoel de Melo obeyed. He sold his business, then locked himself in a room and said, "I'll only open this door after God tells me what to do." He fasted 13 days with no food or water. After midnight on the 13th day, Jesus Himself appeared at the foot of his bed. "Why are you waiting for Me to talk to you?" He asked. "You have my Word in the Bible. Get up and do my work as I have told you to do in My

Word.'' That was March 1955.

Previous to that, de Melo had served the Lord in evangelistic work, preaching on the streets and in organized meetings. But beginning in 1955 he realized that just leaving converts for other churches to follow up was not getting the job done. That is when he began Brazil for Christ as a movement which is essentially based on church planting.

All new Brazil for Christ churches are instructed from the beginning to plant new congregations as a regular part of their ministry. As a result, the average church in the movement has 10 daughter churches which it has planted, and they in turn begin to reproduce immediately.

Each Church One Church

Some might think that, whereas it is easy for big city churches to walk a few blocks and find enough people to form the nucleus of a new daughter church, it is much more difficult to do the same thing in a rural situation. The Assemblies of God in Bolivia, however, is practicing church reproduction out in the country areas of Bolivia's windswept 13,000-foot Altiplano. In the early '70s missionary Bruno Frigoli established a program called ''Each-church-one-church-in-one-year.''

Bolivian Pentecostal pastors agreed to set as a measurable goal the planting of a new church every year. They realized they might not fully be able to accomplish their goal, but they were thinking church growth in a positive and optimistic way. Attractive certificates were printed, one for each year, and churches worked hard to earn a string of certificates to hang on their walls. Whenever a daughter church was formed and organized (in this case 10 baptized believers were required for the nucleus), the mother church received a certificate signed by denominational officers.

The U.S. mission helped some financially in establishing the new churches. The Aymara Indians of the Altiplano are, generally speaking, poor farmers, many still living only on the margin of the money economy. Yet they have found that having a church building is a great help in establishing their testimony in a new village or rancho. So when a new church was organized, the believers there were encouraged to obtain a piece of land, make their own adobe bricks and build the walls of the church building.

Before the mission stepped in, they must also have put on the first half of the galvanized tin roof. The mission then paid for the roofing for the second half, bought the church a supply of literature, and furnished a mule or a bicycle for the pastor in charge, so the pastor could move on to the next village to help plant a new church.

At the end of 1970 the Bolivian assemblies counted only 20 churches. During 1971, 30 new ones were planted, making a total of 50. Each one of the 50 was to plant a new church in 1972. By January 1973 a total of 104 churches reported! The rate of growth for the Assemblies of God in Bolivia increased tremendously through multiplication of churches. An aggressive church planting program turned this denomination around.

Accidental Parenthood

Most of the exciting church planting among Latin American Pentecostals is planned and intentional. That is not the whole picture, however. Many new churches are accidental and unplanned, results of church splits. In their analysis of Pentecostal growth dynamics, Read, Monterroso and Johnson make this revealing comment: "Restructuring often occurs as new dynamic leaders emerge and sometimes clash with the older leaders."[6] One of the outcomes is growth by splitting.

No one will say that church splits are intrinsically good. They frequently involve nasty quarrels and even legal hassles. Often they leave broken hearts and permanent enmities behind. Nevertheless, God promises that "all things work together for good to them that love God" (Rom. 8:28). Church splits among Pentecostals have frequently resulted in accelerated growth for both sides of the split. One might even wonder how the providence of God operates in many of these cases. Perhaps if the churches themselves do not plan for the parenthood of new churches and execute amicable church reproduction, God will allow circumstances to develop which will cause the churches to reproduce by accident.

Since we live in what might be called the "ecumenical age" it is not stylish to attribute any good at all to something as unecumenical as church division, but this does not seem to bother many Pentecostals. In fact, according to historian J. B. A. Kessler, two of Chile's top Pentecostal leaders "do not share the horror for church division which is usually felt in ecumenical circles. In fact both believe that division has helped the astonishing growth of the Pentecostal churches in Chile more than it has hindered it."[7]

This has happened frequently in the Methodist Pentecostal Church. Back in 1946 an aspiring and highly gifted leader, Enrique Chavez, was coming up through the ranks, but the powers that be did not see eye-to-eye with many of his ideas. He was a restless man and did not appreciate being inhibited in his actions. He had gathered a substantial following by then. One thing led to another, and Chavez and his group split off from the Methodist Pentecostal Church to form the new

Pentecostal Church of Chile. Within only 10 years, Chavez had built a huge mother church in Curico which some have likened to a "basilica." Twenty-six daughter churches and 100 others in formation were flourishing.[8] Chavez now claims 100,000 members.

In 1952 it happened again. This time Victor Pavez participated in the splinter group. Within 10 years the new "Pentecostal Church Mission" had grown to 18 churches with a membership of 10,000.[9] It now has 60 churches and 25,000 members.[10] After a careful study, Kessler concludes that the Methodist Pentecostal Church has seen 14 splinter groups move away since the days of Hoover.[11] But, although there have been many painful incidents connected with these splits, they do not seem to have flagged the long-term evangelistic effectiveness either of the mother or of her rebellious daughters.

Biologically speaking, the cells in a healthy body are in a continuous process of division and multiplication. When the body of Christ is healthy, this will occur also. Effective evangelism not only seeks to win individuals and families and peoples to Christ but to plant new churches as frequently as possible. There is nothing particularly Pentecostal about the mother-daughter church pattern. Any church can learn it and put it into practice. Pentecostals in general are doing a magnificent job of it in Latin America, and that is one of the reasons they are reaping such a large proportion of the harvest in those fields which God has whitened.

Chapter Five

Sowing the Seed on Fertile Soil

The "Parable of the Sower" is found in the Bible in Matthew 13, Mark 4 and Luke 8. Curiously, it is one of the least understood parables in the New Testament in spite of the ample space that biblical writers have given it. But seen in proper perspective, it provides us the key to unlock what, in my opinion, is one of the most important factors in the analysis of Pentecostal growth in Latin America. I must confess, however, that this is not a particularly profound observation since church growth research worldwide has shown that *wherever* churches are growing the principle is being applied.

Exactly what is this principle?

It emerges when you attempt to interpret the parable as a farmer would. Today's urban-oriented people have a harder time doing that, perhaps, than did Jesus' disciples who were brought up in a rural setting. When farmers hear anything about sowing and harvesting, they immediately evaluate what is being said in terms of the vision of the fruit. When all is said and done, the thing that ultimately matters to any farmer is the fruit.

The Fruit-Producing Factor

The parable involves a farmer who sowed seed on four kinds of soil. Whether they were separate fields or whether they were all parts of the same field makes no difference. Three of the soils did not produce fruit, but the other did. This is the best place to start in order to understand how the parable relates to church growth, or as Jesus put it, hearing "the word of the kingdom" (Matt. 13:19).

What was the factor that made only one out of four fields produce fruit?

It was not the sower, nor the method, nor the seed, nor the climate. The variable factor was the soil. The seed of the Word of God, like wheat or barley, will produce fruit only when it is wisely sown on fertile soil. No matter how good the seed is, or how dedicated the sower, nothing will grow if the seed falls on a hard roadside. Even prayer will not produce fruit from seed sown on barren ground, any more than prayer will cause oak trees to produce figs.

God, like the farmer, wants fruit. He wants the whitened fields reaped and the sheaves brought to the barn (Matt. 9:37-38). He is not willing that any should perish, but that all should come to repentance (2 Pet. 3:9). Preaching the gospel should bear fruit for eternity. It should make disciples, and thus fulfill God's will as expressed in the Great Commission.

Sowing the seed on barren soil has, unfortunately, become a habit for some. Year after year pastors and evangelists "sow in tears" but they somehow never seem to "reap in joy" (Ps. 126:5), and thus they miss the blessing. As Haggai says, "Ye have sown much, but harvest little" (Hag. 1:6). Years of work sometimes produce a visible fig tree (Luke 13:6-9), but one which bears no fruit. Since it is painful to cut it down, the "work" continues year after year whether it is fruitful or not.

Some pastors and evangelists even come to the point where they attempt to justify barrenness theologically, declaring that it may not be God's will after all that the preaching of the gospel bring men and women to repentance and faith. They thus become addicted to fruitlessness and are to be pitied.

Reaching the Working Class

Fruitlessness, as we have seen, is not a characteristic of Latin American Pentecostals in general. They have found fertile soil, they sow seed there in abundance, and they joyfully reap a harvest. What is this fertile soil? In simple terms it is the working class, the proletariat.

All peoples in Latin America are not equally responsive to the gospel. Some constitute barren soil, as years of hard work and experimentation have shown. But the working class, the disinherited masses, the migrant farmers, the squatters on the fringes of the cities, the poor and oppressed have proved in country after country to be Latin America's fertile soil in the second half of the 20th century. These are the people, generally speaking, that you find in the Pentecostal churches in Latin America.

Sociologists, such as Emilio Willems and Christian Lalive who have studied Pentecostalism from their professional perspective, invariably comment on the proletarian nature of the Pentecostal churches. Without using the term, such writers provide accurate social pointers toward identifying Latin America's fertile soils. In particular, peoples found in the areas of new urbanization and industrialization are receptive to the gospel. In the rural areas Willems found some receptive and some resistant. For example, peasants still under the old hacienda system where the Catholic land owner ruled with an iron hand were least receptive to the Protestant message. Free farmers were only moderately receptive. But those who had been uprooted and relocated in new agricultural areas were found to be highly receptive.[1]

Soils like these are made fertile by the providence of God. There is little way to explain varying degrees of receptivity among peoples without a strong belief in the sovereignty of God. He is known as the Lord of the harvest (Matt. 9:38). Human beings can sow and water, but only God can cause the growth (1 Cor. 3:6-7). Our chief responsibility in evangelistic work is to discern the hand of God in preparing soil or ripening harvests and then to move in, under the power of the Holy Spirit, to sow the seed and gather the sheaves.

Hoover and the Lower Classes

Apparently God was at work in just that way in Chile back in the days of the great Pentecostal revival under Hoover, described in Chapter 1. God used visions and other means to inform His people of His work and will. But when Lalive describes the event from a modern sociologist's point of view, he sees it like this:

"The schism which divided the Methodist Episcopal Church and gave birth to a Chilean Pentecostalism was the result of the opposition between a middle-class ecclesiastical hierarchy, dominated by foreign influence, and the body of believers who were nationals of the lower classes...."[2]

In plainer language, God had prepared the lower class

in Chile for receiving the gospel, but the established Methodist church was not prepared to move in that direction with the aggressive evangelistic program that would bring multitudes of working people into their churches. To think of receiving large numbers of that kind of people was undoubtedly repugnant to many of the middle-class Methodists, although they probably would not have wanted to admit it. It is much easier to react against speaking in tongues and baptisms of fire on the grounds of being "anti-Methodist and anti-biblical" than it is to admit any kind of class preference.

Notice how important the missionary attitude was. Methodists were "dominated by foreign influence," according to Lalive. Further examination, however, will show that the "foreignness" of the missionaries might not have been the chief problem, at least not nearly so much as the social class that the Methodist missionaries belonged to. A very large percentage of missionaries to Latin America have come from the middle class of U.S. or British countries, where the middle class is large. They are typically well-educated and have good manners. This is true not only of Methodists but also of Presbyterians and Baptists and members of the Latin America Mission.

Many churches and missions demand a high degree of cultural and educational polish from their pastors and missionary candidates, some even requiring both college and seminary. These are good qualities, but they do not particularly incline a person toward ministry to the lower classes. When such missionaries arrive in Latin America, they find a very small middle class, but still their natural identification is there so they focus their ministry on that group. Sometimes they discover only too late that they have been assiduously sowing the seed in relatively unproductive soil.

Pentecostalism has traditionally been a religion of the masses in contrast to the classes, even in the affluent countries. Missionaries from U.S. Pentecostal churches find identification with the Latin American masses a natural thing. Those from the more traditional denominations and missions have had an unfortunate tendency to regard Pentecostal missionaries with a degree of contempt because they were not seminary-educated people. Many did not even have a Bible institute diploma. But when all is said and done, the lack of skills in Hebrew, Greek and epistemology may have been more than compensated for by the inherent ability to identify with the working class.

Like begets like. Middle-class missionaries often theorized that their ministry to the middle class would eventually win more of the lower classes. This has not occurred, however, either in Latin America or in other parts of the world. Religious movements in general move from the lower classes up, rather than *vice versa*.

Redemption and Lift

Pentecostals might not have articulated this in such a way, but their social position placed them, predictably, in the midst of the lower class on the mission field. Growth began here, but due to what Donald McGavran calls "redemption and lift"[3] their influence was also eventually felt in the middle class. Reports of an informal survey in Panama, for example, indicate that the Foursquare Church there now counts more well-educated professionals in its membership than the Methodist Church. This is beginning to happen throughout Latin America in general as the century comes to a close.

The "redemption and lift" factor operates when lower-class people are converted, and because of their improved moral life they begin to rise up the social ladder. This can be very detrimental to evangelistic effectiveness if, through it, people lose contact with their former friends, neighbors and relatives. It could have harmed Latin American Pentecostals if they had all risen rapidly to middle-class status and lost contact with the proletariat.

But this has not yet happened to any great degree. The Pentecostal churches have been growing so rapidly that a newly converted first generation of members continues to flood in. This first generation is not particularly concerned with developing "respectability." Their children often are, however, and some of them even leave Pentecostalism to join what they consider more "respectable" churches.

For example, 80 percent of Chilean Pentecostal pastors are first-generation Christians. Lalive comments on this, saying, "...More than half a century after its foundation, Pentecostalism is still in the first-generation period, and may be so for a long time to come."[4] This statement forces us to look toward the future.

Will the most fertile field for future growth in the churches in Latin America continue to be the lower classes? The general consensus is that they will. Australian Methodist Alan Walker says, "That Pentecostalism is touching the poorer millions of Latin America is of deep significance....There is no future for any movement which fails to stir the masses."[5] Pentecostalism will undoubtedly continue to grow as long as it maintains its contact with the masses and thus continues to sow the gospel seed on fertile soil.

As evangelistic strategy is planned for the future in Latin America, the vision of the fruit should be uppermost. Read, Monterroso and Johnson make this remarkable statement:

"While the church is, of course, dedicated to reaching all men, regardless of their class or position, she should concentrate special attention on the masses who are receptive. The future of the church lies with the common people."[6]

Whether this advice will be taken remains to be seen. Middle-class missions and denominations might prove to be slow in changing their status quo. They might continue to feel that carpeted floors, suits and ties, Charles Wesley's hymns, grammatical Spanish, three-point alliterated sermons, dignified worship and pipe organs are values worth preserving whether or not they appeal to the Latin American proletariat. They might feel altogether too uncomfortable with people who bathe only infrequently, have holes in their shoes, spit on the floor, clap when they sing, need a handout now and then and sleep the whole family in a single bedroom. If so, their mediocre growth pattern will probably continue, although some middle- and upper-class peoples are beginning to show receptivity to the gospel.

Pentecostals do not feel these inhibitions and therefore will probably continue to grow among the lower classes.

Chapter Six

Body Life Builds Healthy Churches

When just about every member of the church is active in some ministry or other, the church is bound to grow. To most Pentecostals in Latin America, being a Christian means, among other things, working for God. This is in contrast to more lethargic churches where the pastor and perhaps a deacon or two are virtually the only active workers in the church. Pentecostal pastors often find themselves cast in the enviable role of team coaches. They provide the leadership and the organization, but most of the work out on the streets and in the homes is done by the troops.

While visiting Santiago, Chile, I was once invited by Javier Vasquez, pastor of the Jotabeche Methodist Pentecostal Church, to lead a Bible study with a group of men on Tuesday night. Vasquez referred to them as the "volunteer corps." I was glad to accept the invitation, but I became discouraged when a torrential rainstorm blackened the city late that afternoon. As the meeting time approached it seemed to become worse and worse with spectacular displays of thunder and lightening. By the time I got on and off the bus my shoes were filled with water, and my spirits were as drenched as my clothes. I wondered why I went through with it, for surely no one would come to Bible study.

The Jotabeche Mini-Army

Pastor Vasquez actually did apologize to me for the poor attendance that night. Because of the weather, only about 400 men had come out! The usual attendance, he explained, was at least double that amount. Later on I was amazed to discover that these men had come out to church not only for a Bible study—they had come to receive their instructions as to what each of them was to do for the rest of the week!

Each one was assigned his duties according to his spiritual gifts. The volunteer corps was organized like a mini-army with a clear administrative chain of command so that all were directly accountable to an appointed leader.

Some were sent to minister in jails; some visited hospitals; some called on church members who were having a problem of one kind or another; some preached in open-air meetings; some concentrated their efforts on starting a new congregation; some prayed for the sick; some surveyed a new area to discover whether the people there were responsive to the gospel.

All 400 of them were, in the truest biblical sense of the word, "ministers," actively doing their thing for the Lord. If the paid pastors were the only ministers, Pentecostal churches could not grow as they do. But when all members of the body function together as they should, wonderful things happen.

Body Life

The idea of all members of the body working together has recently been called "body life." The term did not originate either in Latin America or in a Pentecostal church. It comes from Pastor Ray Stedman of the Peninsula Bible Church in Palo Alto, California. Stedman has popularized the phrase in a book by the same title,[1] and the concept is being accepted by an increasing number of Christians. Latin American Pentecostals, however, have been practicing body life for decades, even though they might not use the term as such.

"Body life" describes in a succinct way what 1 Corinthians 12 teaches. The church is compared to a body there—the body of Christ. Christ is the head, and all Christians are members. Every member of the body, when he or she becomes a Christian, is placed in a special position by the Holy Spirit and is expected to function there. In other words, each one is given a spiritual gift. No Christian is allowed to choose his or her own gift; it is assigned by the Holy Spirit. The Christian's responsibility is to discover just what his or her gift is, and then use it for the benefit of the body as a whole.

One of the tragedies of contemporary Christianity is that so many church members have not yet discovered their spiritual gifts and therefore are not using them. Some don't even realize they have one, simply because no one has ever adequately taught them 1 Corinthians 12 or Romans 12. They are, therefore, not able to please the Lord as they should. They are like the timid man in the parable of the talents (Matt. 25:14-30) who buried his talent when he should have been using it. When he met his lord, he was labeled a "wicked, lazy slave" (Matt.25:26). If, somehow, we could dig up and put into use all the buried talents in our Christian churches, I am convinced we would release enough latent spiritual power to win the world for Christ.

The Gift of Evangelist

While it must be admitted that not all Pentecostals in Latin America are doing their part, there is little question that the percentage of those who are is higher in Pentecostal churches than in the slower growing churches. The gift of evangelist is particularly prominent there. Furthermore, all believers are instructed to be aggressive witnesses, whether they have the gift of evangelist or not. The real spiritual hero is the soul winner, the fisher of men. The Holy Spirit gives power to persuade men and women to follow Christ in repentance, faith and baptism, and all Christians are expected to use that power.

The United Pentecostal Church in Pereira, Colombia, for example, has three skilled evangelistic teams organized in its congregation of 310. Each team has 15 members who visit and witness constantly according to well-planned strategy. Often on a Sunday a group of men and women will hire a number of taxis to take them to a neighboring village. They spend the whole day in visitation, saturating the community with the gospel and inviting the responsive people to an evangelistic service in the evening.

When a group of believers is gathered there, the new town becomes a ''preaching point'' and is assigned to a different team for continuing evangelization. The objective is to win new people to Christ and organize a new church as soon as possible.

In a period of only two years the Pereira Church had established 21 preaching points with regular attendance of more than 350, already more than doubling their own church membership.[2]

Evangelistic Methods Will Vary

Methods of effective evangelism differ from place to place. Pentecostals have not succumbed to the danger of institutionalizing a particular evangelistic program. They have not attempted to "package" what may have succeeded in one country and ship it out far and wide, like an exported commodity. The Methodist Pentecostals in Santiago reap abundantly through street preaching, and the Brazil for Christ Church attributes much of its evangelistic fruit to a widespread radio ministry. The *Congregacao Crista* in Brazil knows what others are doing, but they have rejected both street preaching and radio in favor of the individual, person-to-person witness of each member.

The *Congregacao Crista* believes so much in body life that they refuse to hire pastors for their 3,500 churches. They believe that the Holy Spirit provides each church with all the gifts needed for healthy church life, and that when members are properly using their gifts, a professional minister is simply excess baggage. The elders and the deacons do the preaching. The only person the church hires is the bookkeeper; the rest of the work is done by the members themselves.[3]

This is exceedingly effective. The Sao Paulo traffic police are accustomed to regular traffic jams in the Bras area when the *Congregacao Crista* meets on Wednesday and Sunday nights, packing their 3,500-seat auditorium. More traditional churches, where professional, seminary-trained pastors are hired, seem to have few traffic problems.

The point is that, regardless of the method of evangelism which is used, Pentecostal churches have effectively mobilized their members. Notice that not every Pentecostal is equally effective as an evangelist, although everyone is a witness. The whole body is not an eye; if it were, how could it hear (1 Cor. 12:17)? The principle of body life is not that everyone does the same thing, but that everyone does something, according to the gifts the Spirit of God has given.

But whatever any member does, it is geared toward their singular goal of effective evangelism. Not every player on a football team scores points, but everyone plays hard toward that end. Quarterbacks on winning teams make the headlines, but they wouldn't if it weren't for the guards and tackles. Likewise, soul winners make the Pentecostal "headlines," but their effectiveness in frontline evangelism is due to a large extent to the fact that the whole body is healthy and functioning well.

Caring for the New Believers

Part of the action of the body involves instructing new believers. When church growth is rapid, with the Lord adding to the church daily such as should be saved, properly caring for the new believers is altogether impossible if the body life principle is not in effect. More traditional churches, which expect their hired pastoral staffs to take care of the "follow up," have a built-in factor which retards growth. There is no way they can grow adequately, because of a pure and simple lack of manpower.

As we have mentioned previously, the Great Commission not only commands believers to "go" and "make disciples," but also to "baptize" and "teach." Donald McGavran has rephrased these four steps in bucolic terms: seeking, finding, folding and feeding.[4] Evangelism which stops short at either seeking or finding will not result in church growth. The lost sheep must be brought into the fold and properly fed. In churches where conversions and baptisms are counted by the 10s and 20s, this is not a problem for a paid staff to handle. But when they move up into the hundreds and thousands, much more help is needed. Every member of the body needs to do his or her part.

In Colombia, for example, when people are converted through a member of the Assemblies of God, they at once become the center of much attention. Their new brethren in Christ will surround them with love and concern, making sure they begin to attend church regularly. Within a week they are encouraged to join an indoctrination class. Their faith is not allowed to cool. The new lambs are folded and fed. They at once begin to study a special booklet, used all through the denomination, designed to prepare them for baptism and church membership. Right from the beginning, they are taught not only about the church and the Christian life, but they also are introduced to the evangelistic goals of the Assemblies of God. They are taught to be active members of the team, functioning parts of the body.[5]

Pastors and Ministers

When the body life principle is in action, and every Christian is in the biblical sense of the word a "minister," one would expect that the differences between clergy and laity would diminish. This is somewhat true in Latin American Pentecostal churches. It does not mean that paid pastors are rejected by all groups the way they are in the *Congregacao Crista* and some others. The majority of Pentecostal churches do have paid pastors, but this is an application of the body life principle. Generally speaking, Pentecostal pastors have become pastors because of the way God has previously enabled them to function in the body.

Almost invariably, before they become recognized as

77

pastors and hired by the churches, they spent years working as unpaid laypersons. This is in contrast to the more traditional systems such as the Catholic Church which puts young boys in a convent and raises them as priests, or many Protestant churches which choose promising young men and send them through a professional training school such as a Bible institute or seminary *before* they have functioned as active, adult members of the body for a significant time.

Just how this is done will be described in the next chapter, but here it is important to stress that, because of the body life principle, Pentecostals in Latin America have not fallen into an exaggerated professionalization of the clergy as more static churches have done. Pentecostal ministers are really seasoned lay people, and Pentecostal lay people are ministers. It should be no surprise that God is blessing this system. A fresh examination of the pastoral epistles will show that it reflects some valuable biblical principles.

Strong Pastoral Leadership

The more I have studied church growth over 20 years, the more I have come to realize just how key a factor the pastor is for local congregational growth. I had not seen this very clearly when I published the first edition of this book in 1973, and therefore I did not include a section on it. However, further research has indicated that in Latin America, as in other parts of the world, strong pastoral leadership is indeed a vital sign of a healthy church.

Whereas Pentecostals do not have a corner on strong leadership in Latin American evangelical churches, their policy and structure tends toward encouraging it more than that of some other groups. J. B. A. Kessler lists pastoral leadership as the first reason for the amazing growth of Pentecostalism in Chile. He points out that "they have inherited or adopted authoritarian forms of church government." The church expects that the pastor is the leader, and the people are ready to follow. Kessler goes on to say that these forms "may have been dangerous, but were better understood by the nationals than the democratic processes most Protestant missions were trying to introduce."[6]

This helps explain the position of a person like Javier Vasquez, the only full-time salaried pastor of a congregation of something around 100,000, the Jotabeche Methodist Pentecostal Church in Santiago, Chile. There is no thought in his mind that a church could function well with more than one pastor. Vasquez says, "You can't have two heads to a body."[7] The authority he exercises is hard for more traditionally and democratically oriented North Americans to comprehend. But it is no problem to the church members there who perceive Vasquez to be their servant.

A thorough study of Latin American evangelical leadership was recently done by Philip Thornton of Asbury College. He found that the strong *caudillo* type leadership was characteristic of growing, healthy churches largely because "these spiritual *caudillos* were giving leadership to their urban congregations in a culturally appropriate manner." The successful leaders whom Thornton studied were good motivators of their people; they were positive and clear; they held strong opinions; and "they projected an air of confidence that was contagious among their followers."[8]

Paulo Macalao was pastor of the Madureira Assembly of God in Rio de Janeiro for 50 years until his recent death. During that time the church grew to 18,500 members including the mother church and 120 satellite daughter churches. Pastor Macalao was the leader, a spiritual *caudillo* type who was in control of the whole structure. Under his authority were 100 associate pastors, 180 evangelists, 300 elders and 3,600 deacons. Three new satellite churches began every year, and Macalao, with the advice of his council of pastors, appointed new pastors for them. All major decisions were approved by Macalao. How did he maintain control, since this is a voluntary association? The church members looked to him as anointed of God, and they had no inclination to question his authority. Macalao once said, "We do not beat them, but they obey."[9]

The anointing is very important to Pentecostals. In Chapter 4 I told the story about Manoel de Melo's hair-raising experience with a runaway automobile and the voice of God coming directly to him. This sort of contact with the supernatural lends itself to a high degree of confidence in one's call to the ministry. Non-Pentecostal denominations which are uncomfortable with contemporary prophecy tend not to trust direct contact with the Holy Spirit and thereby build in a system of checks and balances which tend to siphon off authority from the pastoral office. Most do not know that this reduces the growth potential of their churches.

Christian Lalive points out that the Pentecostals he studied in Chile not only believe that their pastors are divinely appointed, but that the resulting authoritarian *caudillo* structure which emerged is also understood by them as the most biblical pattern. They see the biblical model which "speaks of shepherd, father, master, patriarch, and puts forth a relationship of love, naturally, but an imperious love." Culturally, the colonial pattern of the *hacienda* with the owner as the leader and protector of all the workers is also reflected in Pentecostal church leadership patterns. Put this together and "one may say that the Pentecostal leader performs his role according to the Chilean tradition of authority, but he himself will, with justice, claim to be following the biblical tradition."[10] That is a winning combination.

It may seem at first glance that the strong, authoritative leadership style characteristic of Pentecostal pastors contradicts the first part of this chapter which emphasizes body life and the vital role of lay people in Pentecostal church growth. This would be the case if the pastors expected themselves to do all the ministry in the church. But they do not. They fully expect the ministry of the church to be done by lay people who are active in discovering, developing and using their spiritual gifts.

With a combination of strong pastoral leadership and strong lay ministry, Latin American Pentecostals have discovered a formula which has helped catapult them to sustained church growth.

Chapter Seven

Seminaries in the Streets

Several times now we have mentioned the Jotabeche Methodist Pentecostal Church of Santiago, Chile. This offspring of the revival under Hoover in 1909 has developed into a microcosm of much of Latin American Pentecostalism. It has the largest membership and the largest sanctuary, seating 16,000. Their membership is active, their worship service is exciting, and the power of God is evident among them. All in all, it is one of the truly typical Pentecostal churches on the continent.

Javier Vasquez

The reason for stressing this is to introduce the pastor of the Jotabeche Church, Javier Vasquez. Vasquez is a man of 60, of medium build, with straight black hair and a strong, square jaw. His movements, like his words, are slow and deliberate. His air is serious, although he has a ready smile. He dresses conservatively in a dark suit, white shirt and dark tie with little concern for style or tailoring. His whole appearance and manner identify him with the common people who make up his congregation.

Although he is little known outside of Chile, Javier Vasquez is without doubt one of the most significant church leaders in Christendom. I have not been able to confirm this to my entire satisfaction, but information from reliable sources claims that when Vasquez was elected pastor of the Jotabeche Church, he received 40,000 secret-ballot votes. These would have come not only from members of the mother church, but also from the multiple daughter churches scattered all over the capital city. Even so, few pastors I can think of in the United States could claim even 10 percent of that number of votes behind their pastoral call.

To provide the leadership for such an enormous church, Vasquez needs well-seasoned pastoral and administrative gifts. On the platform, he needs the charisma to handle the huge crowd, allowing them the proper measure of freedom of expression balanced with the discipline which will keep them attentive during the sermon. He does his job well and is loved by his people.

I have no details as to Vasquez' financial condition. By all outward appearances, he is a humble man who lives unostentatiously. Undoubtedly, however, he is taken care of adequately. David Brackenridge gives a notable description of the typical Pentecostal pastor:

"It is astonishing to note the care and reverence the people show toward their pastor. Everything is done for him. Besides monetary support, members bring gifts of meat, vegetables, and fruit. His table is usually full. He entertains lavishly, and no member is turned away who is in need. But it must be said that the pastor controls everything—finances and all the activities. Nothing is done without his consent."[1]

Where Did You Go to Seminary?

How are pastors like Javier Vasquez trained? Where do they learn to preach and carry such heavy pastoral responsibility? Uninitiated visitors have asked Vasquez where he went to seminary. He answers without hesitation, "Out there in the streets. I would want no other."

Is this sour grapes? Not for Vasquez. He is well enough known abroad to have been offered lavish study scholarships. He undoubtedly could pick his institution if he wanted to take further study almost any place in the world. But although he might not articulate it with any great fluency, intuitively he knows that more important than all the academic honors and degrees in Europe or the United States is maintaining identification with the people God has called him to minister to.

It is not that Vasquez has never seen churches which insist on seminary-trained pastors. Santiago has scores of them, and Vasquez rubs shoulders with the ministers. While he is humble enough to admit that he needs to know more Bible and theology, he is realistic enough to see that seminary training has its negative, as well as positive, effects there in his Latin American context. Vasquez notices that many of the churches with highly trained pastors are meeting the needs of only a very few people; they continually struggle with program after program to keep "relevant"; their services are dull and uninviting; their balance sheets show an excessive amount of red ink, and their evangelistic impact is minimal.

Even though other pastors make close friends with government officials, enjoy expense-paid jaunts abroad to prestigious international conferences, debate theology and social ethics on academic levels, speak English fluently and publish scholarly articles in ecclesiastical journals, Pentecostal pastors like Vasquez do not feel in the least envious. Nor do they spend much time criticizing the others. They just keep on with what they know is God's calling for them—bringing multitudes of Chileans to repentance and faith in Jesus Christ.

Why Institutions Are Resisted

While Pentecostal pastors might not be able to discuss the history and philosophy of theological education on a level with men like Ted Ward and Bobby Clinton, they do raise similar questions. For one thing, they ask whether the slow growth of non-Pentecostal churches might in fact have something to do with the way their ministers are trained. They tend to think it might, and therefore they are not generally anxious to change. Many outsiders have offered to "help" them with funds, personnel and know-how. Such groups as the World Council of Churches, some faith missions, newer denominations and others would set up a seminary program for them at the drop of a hat, but the Pentecostals have, until very recently, staunchly refused.

A recent study of the Protestant clergy in Chile has brought some remarkable facts to the surface.[2] Non-Pentecostal pastors are divided 50-50 according to age: half are over 40 and half are under 40. But a full 82 percent of Pentecostal pastors are over 40 years of age. In the category of under 30, the non-Pentecostals have 23 percent of their pastors, while Pentecostals have only 3 percent. In other words, Pentecostal pastors are for the most part older, experienced persons.

Even more revealing, perhaps, is the comparison of educational levels. No non-Pentecostal pastors of those surveyed had less than full primary education. But 56 percent of the Pentecostal pastors had not finished primary school. Apparently, then, academic achievement is not considered by Pentecostals in Latin America as an important qualification for the ministry.

Redemption and Lift

One other aspect of the survey will help our understanding of Pentecostal ministers. Of the non-Pentecostal pastors, 78 percent were second-generation Protestants, while Pentecostals reverse the ratio with 79 percent first-generation Christians, converted from the world. Think of what this means. We see here what is most likely a demonstration of Donald McGavran's theory of "redemption and lift."[3] Christian redemption so cleans up the personal life and so changes human values, that often it will lift a family from a lower social class to the middle class. This is good, so long as the lifted family does not lose contact with the masses and disqualify themselves from winning their friends and relatives to Christ.

Redeemed people, generally speaking, adopt new educational values. They say, "I want my children to have the advantages I missed." They encourage their children to go through secondary school and a university. In other words, they want their children to have a middle-class education, marry a middle-class spouse and live in a middle-class neighborhood. There is nothing wrong with this, and one could hardly wish anything else for fellow believers in Christ.

But whenever this happens, one should not be surprised that the *evangelistic effectiveness* of these second-generation people is drastically reduced. To pick up the terminology from Chapter 5, they have moved from fertile soil (the masses) to relatively barren soil (the classes). Among other things, they have also virtually disqualified themselves from being grass-roots

Pentecostal pastors.

The study we have been referring to confirms this theory of redemption and lift.[4] It shows that there is virtually no difference between the social class origins of Pentecostal and non-Pentecostal pastors. About 70 percent of all pastors were born into lower-class homes. But because most non-Pentecostal pastors were raised in Christian homes, they were converted as young people. They then had more educational advantages, and they tended to lose contact with the fertile field of the lower class where they were born. Pentecostal pastors, on the other hand, were converted as adults and never made a radical break from their social contacts.

Why the Streets Are Superior

With this profile of Pentecostal pastors, we can better understand both how they are trained and how this training helps Pentecostal churches to grow. Some outsiders, when they first hear about them, feel sorry for Pentecostal pastors and their "seminaries in the streets." But further examination reveals that this is in all probability a surprisingly high quality of training for the pastorate. As a matter of fact, it may well be that people from the outside who, with a generous heart, advocate reform in this area, might unwittingly be cutting away at one of the tap roots of Latin American Pentecostalism. It would be a shame if the desire for more educational respectability in the Pentecostal ministry eventually stalled Pentecostal church growth.

Candidates for the Pentecostal street seminaries look much more like the description of Christian leaders in 1 Timothy than the average student in a traditional seminary. Since they are older, they can be judged as candidates for the pastorate, not on what they *might be* when they get older, but on what they have *proven to be*. They have a spouse and a family whom they govern well; they are not novices; they are patient, sober-minded and temperate. Moreover, they have a good report by those who are outside the fellowship, something that younger persons who have not yet made an adult contribution to society can hardly claim.

These Christian leaders who have been gifted by God for the pastorate are not sent far away to some institution for three years or so. They stay with their families; they work at their jobs; they keep their social contacts; they worship with their people; and through all this they learn by doing. They learn their skills like craftsmen through the ages have learned—by apprenticeship. They feel that the best place to learn how to be a pastor is with pastor and people, not so much with theologians and scholars.

Street Seminaries Are Not Easy

The apprenticeship system actually makes becoming a pastor a more difficult procedure than does a traditional seminary education. Success in the ministry itself becomes the qualifying factor, not the awarding of a diploma or a degree. The final exam is confirmation through actual experience that God has given the appropriate gifts, and that the candidate, through the power of the Holy Spirit, knows how to exercise them effectively.

There is no stereotyped system that all Pentecostal churches in Latin America follow for training their pastors. Almost all of them, however, involve apprenticeship in one way or another. Those who become pastors typically have had an abundance of previous experience in all aspects of church work, but different Pentecostal churches use different titles for their leaders. Here is one of the typical ladders which lead up to the status of pastor in a Pentecostal church:

1. *Street preacher.* As I pointed out in Chapter 3, every convert is expected to be a witness for Christ, and in some cases they must go out in the street the following Sunday to give their testimony in public. This means that all believers are candidates for this first rung of the ladder, and therefore all have some possibility of the pastorate before them. Experience will soon reveal which of the believers who give their testimonies in the streets have the gifts to preach regularly, and the successful ones may move up to the next rung.

2. *Sunday school teacher.* Some Pentecostal churches have Sunday school, and some don't. But all have Bible classes of one kind or another, and those who show up well in the street are invited to take a class. If the teachers find they can communicate simple Bible truths to their students and hold the interest of the class, they pass this test and go up another rung.

3. *Preacher.* When the pastor asks one of his people to be a "preacher," this means being permitted to lead worship services and occasionally taking the sermon in smaller meetings. If the apprentice shows ability in this ministry and the pastor is pleased with the performance, the next rung of the ladder is:

4. *New preaching point.* When the candidates are sent out by the pastor to new preaching points, they carry a heavier responsibility. They must evangelize an assigned area, and their success is measured by nothing less than converts. If, through their ministry, men and women are coming to faith in Christ and transformed lives are evident, this is interpreted as the will of God that they obtain official recognition by the denomination. The next rung up is the first "official" position.

5. *Christian worker.* In order to become an official

Christian worker, the pastor must present the candidate's name to the annual conference with a recommendation. This step is taken seriously, and by no means do all those who enter the apprentice system of training make it this far. Many remain in the ranks, doing their best for the Lord. Christian workers come under the authority of denominational leadership, and wider ministries begin to open outside the sphere of influence of the local church.

6. *Pastor-deacon.* Once the Christian workers are promoted to pastor-deacon, they are usually assigned a new area of the city or village where they are expected to plant new churches. In fact, planting a new church is a requirement for confirmation on this rung of the ladder. If they cannot do this successfully, they rise no further and do not make the category of pastor, the final rung.

7. *Pastor.* The annual conference takes the action of naming probationers to full pastor only when they are tested and found true. Here the test involves economics. Not only must they plant a church, but they must nurture it until it becomes large and solvent enough to support them financially as pastor. When pastors can present sufficient evidence that they can leave their secular employment to dedicate themselves entirely to the pastorate, they are awarded the title.

There is no set time for the journey up the ladder. Young people might spend 15 or 20 years at it until their maturity and leadership ability have been accepted by the churches. This apprenticeship system sifts and sorts until people who fit biblical patterns of leadership emerge. It does not pass older persons by as do some traditional theological training institutions. One man was converted at the age of 58 in a Pentecostal church in

Nicaragua. He was gifted for the pastorate, and the Assemblies of God there had a training program which he entered at age 60. For the next 15 years he served effectively as pastor of a Nicaraguan church.[5]

Where Pentecostals do have the more traditional type of Bible institutes, they still are characterized by a flexibility that builds in the type of training we have described. Theoretical training or knowledge for its own sake has no place there. All training is functional, geared for effectiveness in the ministry.

One Pentecostal Bible institute in Central America has been highly productive as a center for evangelism and church planting for many years. Its requirements for graduation are unusual, but effective in extending the kingdom of God. The institute admits first-year students even if they have little or no experience in the ministry, but when that year is over, they are sent to a new field to plant a church. They can only be readmitted for further studies after they have successfully planted a church, which in turn is able to support them in their continuing education. By that time, they have become experienced workers and they are much more highly motivated to learn.

A Danger Sign

Seminaries in the streets have been so successful in training Pentecostal leadership in Latin America that one would expect them to be a permanent fixture. However, the formal educational establishment is inexorable. Once a few Pentecostal leaders manage to bypass the system and attend formal seminaries or Bible colleges either in Chile or abroad and then work their way back into the structures of the Pentecostal churches, new items begin to appear on the agendas of church conventions and councils. Some argue that ''we must upgrade our ministry." They say, "If our pastors don't go to seminary, how can they minister to the increasing number of university students and college-trained professionals?"

It is my observation that institutionalizing pastoral training can be one of the sure signs that a vital grassroots Christian movement is running out of steam. Several American Pentecostal denominations have recently backed a project to establish a Pentecostal Bible institute in Chile, designed to take pastoral training off the streets and put it in the classroom where they feel it belongs. This in itself may not be a hindrance to church growth in the near future especially if modern technology for leadership selection and training is sensitively applied. But it could also be a danger.

Much of the current top Pentecostal leadership recognizes the danger and is trying to keep their training to the apprenticeship system. It is difficult to know what the future holds. I hope it does not hold a two-tiered training system which will give first-class status to pastors who have graduated from the Bible institute and second-class status to those who haven't. My hunch would be that, measured by effectiveness in leading churches to growth, the first-class pastors for some time to come will be those who went to seminary out there in the streets.

Chapter Eight

It's Fun to Go to Church

Emilio Castro, a Uruguayan Methodist leader, is now general secretary of the World Council of Churches. As a world class Christian leader, Castro can see significant trends. This statement of Castro's has important implications for discovering the secrets of Pentecostal growth in Latin America:

"It is safe to say that Pentecostalism is probably the most "indigenous" Latin American kind of Pentecostalism....Because they are not institutionally bound to churches in other parts of the world...and consequently are not economically dependent on foreign groups—Pentecostal churches may be said to represent authentic Latin American Protestantism."[1]

Indigenous Pentecostal Churches

The remarkable way that Pentecostal churches have been able to take on the shape of the culture in which they are growing gives Pentecostals an appeal that other churches seem to attain only with great difficulty. Generally speaking, Pentecostals have become more indigenous to Latin America than liberals on the one hand and fundamentalists on the other. Foreign influence and control have been minimal in the development of Latin American Pentecostalism. While it is true that missionaries were involved in planting the Pentecostal churches at first, the subsequent growth of the churches was in many cases so rapid that the foreigners could not have controlled the national churches even if they had wanted to.

Missionary paternalism is much more likely to occur in situations of slow growth. Ten missionary couples can have an overbearing influence on a church of 100 members, and this influence will be felt no matter how hard the missionaries try to avoid it. But when the 10 couples are working alongside a church of 100,000, it is a different story. In a large, growing church, even a "great white father" type of missionary can rarely succeed in dominating the church.

In Chile, Willis Hoover exercised considerable influence over the Methodist Pentecostal Church while he was alive. But happily he did not build a missionary empire. He did not recruit other foreigners to take his place. He did not feel that the nationals were incapable of leading the church. "Since Hoover's time," J. B. A. Kessler says, "no more foreigners have been connected with the indigenous Pentecostal movement, and all negative nationalism has of itself come to an end."[2]

Many non-Pentecostal missions have been much slower to turn over new churches to national leaders. This lingering paternalism almost invariably produces two results which retard church growth. The first is a foreignness about the church so that it appears to be something both exotic and irrelevant to unbelievers. The second is the development of a strong anti-missionary sentiment, particularly in second-generation believers.

The syndrome of church development creeps up so subtly that missions often do not recognize that they should have taken their hands off church affairs long ago. Then when the tensions between missionaries and nationals build up to the breaking point, the turnover becomes a traumatic experience with the outbreak of severe nationalism, wounded personal feelings on both sides, and consequent slow growth. Human energies, both missionary and national, are dissipated on internal troubleshooting rather than on winning the world to Christ.

Trusting the Holy Spirit

The ability of Pentecostal missions to turn God's work willingly over to nationals might possibly be traced to their strong emphasis on the Holy Spirit. The Bible promises that the Holy Spirit will guide believers of whatever nationality into all truth (John 16:13), and Pentecostal missionaries are more likely to take that literally than others might be. In the final analysis, they do not let their decision as to turning over the work depend so much on whether they can trust their national brethren as to whether they can trust the Holy Spirit. In this area the Pentecostal trust index is high.

Non-Pentecostal missionaries sometimes are unable to recognize that educational standards can insidiously substitute for simple trust in the Holy Spirit. The cliche that "my job is to work myself out of a job" is the cause of some of these problems. The missionary who says this tends to think in terms of a national *replacing a missionary* as over against a national *leading his own church*. There is a tremendous difference between the two, especially for a missionary who belongs to a mission which is proud of "keeping its educational standards high." The missionaries all have had primary and secondary schooling, followed by Bible college or university and even in some cases seminary. When they go on furlough, the mission almost by reflex action replaces them with an equally well-trained missionary.

The operation of cultural overhang here is obvious. In an effort to exhibit Christian humility, the missionary says, "I wish I could do a better job. I could if I had more training. The training I have had only barely qualifies me for my job." Having said this, and combining it with the compulsion to train nationals to take over the missionary's job, the missionary is caught in a web. He or she must see to it that the nationals at the very least attain the missionary's own standards, so they develop programs for primary and secondary school, Bible institute, and seminary. In some cases missionaries even aspire to send national leaders abroad for the final polish, most frequently to their own country and to their own alma maters. When this happens (and if by some miracle the nationals do not join the "brain drain" in the process), the missionaries feel they can turn some of the work over.

Then the surprise comes. The years and years this process has taken have deeply encrusted missionary paternalism into the church. Educational standards have been imposed which are foreign to the culture of the church members. Institutions have been developed to meet these standards which can only be staffed and financed by missionaries, and these have now become an integral part of the church. Academic degrees have unconsciously been elevated above Holy Spirit gifts and power. The church development syndrome has again run its course. If the missionaries were to pull out completely, it is questionable if the church could survive.

Happily, not all non-Pentecostal churches in Latin America are like the stereotype I have just described. But enough are to make this a widespread problem and one that honest missionaries will immediately acknowledge. There is little hope that a church like this can become significantly indigenous, at least within the present generation.

Music and Liturgy

Foreign ways of doing things have been deeply associated in the minds of the nationals themselves with spiritual Christianity. Hymns by Fanny Crosby and Isaac Watts, played on pianos and organs, may come to be considered *more spiritual* than those written by nationals to national music rhythms and played on guitars and maracas, incredible as that may seem. Music that pleases the ear and makes the foot tap, regardless of how eloquently the lyrics praise God, is considered worldly, not only by missionaries, but also by some nationals!

Church music is a part of liturgy. The word liturgy is sometimes closely associated with very ritualistic churches, but it need not be. In its broadest sense, it simply means the form a church has chosen to use to worship God.

What I have been leading up to so far is this: largely because Pentecostal churches have been allowed to become indigenous very early in their development, they have developed a culturally relevant liturgy. This is one important reason why Pentecostal churches are growing.

Worship Without Yawns

One of the first things you notice when you go into a worship service in a Latin American Pentecostal church is how much the people seem to be enjoying themselves. The hardest thing to find in one of the Pentecostal services is a wide yawn. Unfortunately, yawns are all too common in many other churches in Latin America. Services are boring, and for many it is a chore to go to church once or twice on Sunday, but it is a Christian exercise that must be taken, so the faithful put up with it.

The problem is that, while believers might have enough self-motivation to fulfill their weekly obligation, they are reluctant to invite their unsaved friends and neighbors to participate. They know by experience that their dull liturgy turns off the average Latin American, and consequently evangelism becomes difficult and ineffective.

But since Pentecostals have fun going to church, they do not hesitate to bring others along. They know ahead of time that when they lead other people to Christ, they can bring those newborn babes to a spiritual home they will enjoy. The Pentecostal community is Latin American enough in every way to make Latin Americans feel at home. Culturally relevant liturgy thus becomes a strong growth factor.

What does Latin American Pentecostal liturgy look like? In order to answer this question, I have classified the most important elements under eight headings:

1. The Bigness

Size in itself can produce very beneficial psychological results. This is the "rally" aspect of church life. Bigness is at times threatening because bigness can work against another equally important aspect of church life—the community. If, along with bigness, the church does not provide structures through which Christians can form intimate relationships with each other, where they can hurt together and bleed together and rejoice together and encourage one another on the gut level, then size itself is worthless. But this community aspect of Latin American Pentecostalism is described in other chapters. Here our attention is on what Pentecostals do when they all come together to worship.

When unbelievers walk into the Portales Church in Mexico City or the Brazil for Christ Church in Sao Paulo or the Hidalgo Church in Buenos Aires or the Jotabeche Church in Santiago, they know they are in the midst of something highly unusual. Literally thousands of people gathering together weekly at the same time in the same place, not for a soccer game or a bull fight or a political demonstration, but to worship God, is an attractive spectacle. In a real sense it is an effective evangelistic tool.

But not only is it appealing to unbelievers, it helps build up the believers and strengthens their faith. Believers feel as if they are winners. They develop positive thinking and benefit from the power that accompanies it. They are encouraged when they know they are part of something big. When they go out into the world, they go with a self-confidence and optimism that radiates to others and makes them more effective in their witness than they might otherwise be.

Howard Snyder has described the effect of the bigness of the Brazil for Christ Church in Sao Paulo in these graphic terms:

"Packing into the public buses, perhaps singing as they come, they converge on their temple. From all parts of the city and outlying areas they come, ready to share the joy and excitement of a great throng of believers on Saturday night. They pray, sing, witness, and hear their leader. Tomorrow they will be scattered in hundreds of congregations around the city, many of which are small and struggling. But they will not be discouraged: they know they are part of a people, a movement! Something is happening, something big, something God-sized. They have seen it and felt it."[3]

Bigness helps generate the power to produce more bigness.

2. The Social Opportunity

Believers in the Pentecostal churches are not anonymous. They relate to each other well. Many arrive a full half hour before the service starts in order to see their friends, exchange warm *abrazos*, inquire about the health of their families and share experiences. This social free-for-all is more reminiscent of a railroad station than Westminster Cathedral, but it makes sense to Latin Americans who by nature are much more personable and emotional than Anglo-Saxons.

Latin American churches which suffer from the cultural overhang of their Anglo-Saxon founders are somber by contrast. They have been taught that, in the period before the worship service begins, "the Lord is in His holy temple; let all the earth keep silence before Him." A fun time of social mixing in the sanctuary is regarded as unspiritual and a violation of true worship. They insist that you come to church to talk to God, not to each other.

3. The Noise Level

Christians who feel this way about church also tend to feel that when you talk to God you should do so quietly. Prayer is most typically either led by the minister in a well-modulated voice, or designated as a "time of silent prayer." In other words, the noise level in the average non-Pentecostal church is very similar to any church you would find in Scotland or Scandinavia or South Dakota. A baby's whimper becomes a major distraction.

Pentecostals in Latin America don't feel this way about church, however. Even in times of prayer, the noise level is high. Simultaneous prayer is common practice. When it comes time for talking to God, everybody in the room talks to Him, and the noise rises to a loud roar. The exuberant worshippers do not feel particularly inhibited about their own voice levels either, and some actually shout at the top of their lungs while they are praying.

Is this unspiritual? Hardly. Hundreds of people addressing God together must be some sort of a highly spiritual exercise. Does it aid worship? Yes. It has many beneficial effects on the type of people who are doing it. It produces a sense of high drama; it nourishes the emotions; and it makes the presence of God more real to believers. Anthropologist Eugene Nida has observed that this even *helps* people to pray, since it brings prayer from the semi-professional level found in many churches to the level of the common person.

Everybody is invited to pray, and "the contagion is such that one can scarcely avoid praying."[4] Many who would never dare to pray when everyone else was listening lose their timidity and gladly pray when everyone else is doing the same. Mistakes in grammar or lack of ecclesiastical polish are not even noticed by the person in the next seat. To God, they are not important at all.

At times the noise and excitement have caused problems. A few years ago in Puerto Rico the Pentecostal Church of Old San Juan was taken to court. Neighbors complained that the loud singing, the handclapping, the musical instruments, the shouting "Hallelujah" and falling on the floor caused a "public nuisance." They claimed that it interfered with watching TV and children studying. As it went through court, many wondered out loud why the neighboring barrooms with jukeboxes blaring weren't also taken to court. But to no avail. The church had to pay $1,500 in damages to the neighbors. But with all that it kept growing, and the Pentecostals kept having a good time.

4. The Participation

Hardly anybody keeps track of how many persons might actually participate in a typical Pentecostal service, but Ed Murphy took the trouble to count them at a service in Colombia and came up with a total of 65 participants. He speculates that "if missionaries would have had their hand in this, it is unlikely the service would have followed the course it did."[5] It is highly unlikely, because that is not the way Anglo-Saxons usually do things.

For one thing, the high quality professional training and subsequent gulf between clergy and laity that many Anglo-Saxon churches have been living with for generations have tended to cast all responsibility for leading worship on one person, the pastor. Some churches have even had to develop a "Lay People's Sunday" in a pathetic attempt to remedy the situation.

Pentecostal worshippers who do not participate in a direct way participate indirectly, but nevertheless actively. Worship is anything but a passive experience. It is people-centered rather than platform-centered. The audience participates with "Amen" and "Hallelujah" and "Praise the Lord." The Chilean Pentecostals are well-known for their three-fold "Glory to God." Several times during the average service the opportunity will come for the audience to spring to its feet, throw its arms up into the air and shout with full volume, "Gloria a Dios," three times. The total dramatic effect is breathtaking. To be honest, it's fun!

5. The Motion

One thing that reduces yawns in Pentecostal churches is the need to keep moving. Worshippers stand up and sit down so frequently that no one settles back enough to get sleepy. Lifting hands up and down also keeps the pulse beating.

In Chile the Methodist Pentecostals have even designed a unique kind of pew to allow for another motion—kneeling to pray. Crowded conditions push the pews so close together that there would not be room enough to kneel, if it weren't for the movable backs on the benches. When the signal is given, the congregation kneels, and everyone pushes on the back of the bench ahead of them. It is so hinged that it moves forward and provides a space for your elbows while you pray. You have to move fast in order not to get slapped across the back by your own bench. The resulting clackity-clack of hundreds of pew backs contributes to the noise level and thus to the drama of the service.

To increase motion, some of the Pentecostal churches do not send ushers up and down the aisles with offering plates, but rather invite the givers to come forward and lay their offerings on the altar up in the front of the church. While they are doing it the choir might be singing a special number, or the audience might be singing. At first it looks like a violation of the "decently and in order" clause of Paul's instructions to the Corinthians (1 Cor. 14:40), but it isn't. It is a carefully planned and well-disciplined aspect of the Pentecostal liturgical pattern. It is part of the very decency and order that is most relevant to them.

Spiritual dancing introduces a kind of motion into the worship services that the newcomer considers unusual at first, but later finds to be quite enchanting. Ordinarily during congregational singing or during a choir number, several individuals will begin dancing right in their pews, moving their arms and bodies with varying degrees of gracefulness. Some will find their way to the aisles or to open spaces at the back or front of the church. I once saw what must be the most unusual sign ever posted on the wall of a church: "Dancing on the stairs prohibited." This was just another indication that not only order, but also physical safety, is a concern of Pentecostal brethren.

6. Tongues

Speaking in tongues is so commonplace in Pentecostal services in Latin America that some of them might wonder why it is listed here as a separate item. Most speaking in tongues occurs during prayer times, so it might more naturally be included as an item under prayer. But since this is being written for non-Pentecostals as well as for Pentecostals, one or two things need to be said about this.

For many members of the working class in Latin America, life can easily become a dull, colorless routine. With little excess money to spend on household conveniences, automobiles, vacations or entertainment, exciting moments that lift a person above the monotonous humdrum of daily existence are few. In the world they are often compensated for in drunkennesss, brawling and loose living. Many, however, have found that Christianity offers them a similar release and that worshipping God can even become ecstatic. The gift of tongues produces much spiritual satisfaction for many people, and non-Pentecostals should be cautious, as Paul himself recommends, about forbidding others to speak in tongues (1 Cor. 14:39).

How does speaking in tongues happen? Here is a firsthand testimony of a Latin American Pentecostal, which might well be considered typical of the tongues experience:

"One time I was praying in a meeting. I believed very little in this matter of tongues and had doubts. But on May 20, 1967, in a prayer meeting in church, as I was praying in a very concentrated way, all of a sudden I felt as if someone had turned a very strong searchlight on me and I was burning. I was going to speak in Spanish, but couldn't. I couldn't see anything but flames of fire all around me, and I felt as if I were burning. Then I began to speak in tongues—I was conscious, but I was in ecstasy."[6]

Some non-Pentecostals do forbid speaking in tongues on the grounds that they are not an appropriate gift for the church today. The Scofield Bible, which has been translated into Spanish, says in its note on 1 Corinthians 14:1 that "tongues and sign gifts are to cease," and many sincere evangelicals believe it. It is not my purpose here to argue whether they are right or wrong. They are entitled to their opinion, although their attitude toward those who disagree with them should be one of love and tolerance.

But others say that while tongues might be appropriate today, Pentecostals in Latin America are abusing them like the Corinthians did, and to that degree they need to be reprimanded and corrected. Whether they are or not is largely a matter of personal judgment. My own opinion is that for the most part this is not true. My understanding of the problem dealt with in 1 Corinthians 12-14 is that the Corinthians were dividing Christians into first-class and second-class categories on the basis of whether they had the gift of tongues or not.

The Corinthians' mistake was that they tended to make tongues the most important spiritual gift, a mistake which I personally have not observed in a general way among Latin American Pentecostals, although obviously the temptation to fall into that error is there, and cases might be cited to prove that some have gone off that deep end. Where this has happened, someone does need to exhort and reprimand these brethren, but in the Spirit.

Also, according to 1 Corinthians 14, tongues must be accompanied by interpretation if they are used as a vehicle of communicating truths from God to the congregation as prophecy also does. This is true, but Paul goes on to say that if no interpreter is present, tongues should be used "to speak to himself and to God" (1 Cor. 14:28). My understanding is that this is exactly what Pentecostals are doing when they pray in unison, some praying in tongues. They could do the same thing equally as effectively if they were at home in their private devotions, but the instructions in 1 Corinthians could hardly be limited to that.

So much for my brief apology for tongues in the Pentecostal liturgy. Let me simply repeat what I have said before: just because the Pentecostals do it, it doesn't mean that all Christians have to do it. Experience has shown that tongues are beyond doubt the most threatening aspect of Pentecostalism for non-Pentecostals. All right, even without tongues (which constitutes only one of eight sub-points in only one chapter of this book), Pentecostals have discovered many other secrets of church growth that can be applied by Christians who prefer not to speak in tongues. If only because of tongues someone says, "I want nothing to do with the Pentecostals," I'm afraid they have thrown out the baby with the bath water.

7. The Music

One of the most unreal things I saw when I was first being introduced to Latin American Pentecostalism was an orchestra of about 500 members with the basic instruments being guitars, mandolins and accordions. Not a pipe organ in the place! But a pipe organ never sounded like those 500 instruments!

Some will respond that they prefer a pipe organ in church any time. I would agree, as long as pipe organs are producing culturally relevant liturgies that draw people to the church and to Jesus Christ. To many Latin Americans, guitars and accordions are more attractive than pipe organs. It would be extremely difficult to classify one more "biblical" than the other. A more important question is: which sounds better to our people?

Clapping the hands in rhythm to the music is common in Pentecostal services in Latin America. This increases personal participation in the liturgy, raises the noise level several decibels and heightens the tone of the drama. One of the severe structural problems that the Brazilian architects encountered while building the gigantic 10,000-seat auditorium for the Brazil for Christ Church in Sao Paulo related directly to this. The roof had to be designed with more than average care. If the huge span were to cover an airplane hangar or a warehouse it wouldn't have been that difficult. But the sound waves from 10,000 Brazilian Pentecostals clapping in unison could have produced the effect of troops marching over a bridge.

Indigenous Pentecostal hymnology is developing at different rates in different places. There is no such thing as a uniform Latin American musical style. Mexican,

Bolivian, Brazilian and Argentine music is all quite distinct. Some Pentecostal groups are working on this, but perhaps not as rapidly as one might expect. Even so, the translations of some of the Anglo-Saxon hymns are often sung to a Latin beat that might stun Charles Wesley if he were to hear what has happened to his music.

8. The Preaching

Pentecostal preaching in Latin America is quite distinct from monologues which characterize most of the traditional churches. The Pentecostal preacher enters into a kind of dialogue with the audience. The sermon is an experience for those who listen, as they respond with loud shouts of approval which surge up like waves breaking over the seashore. The preachers know just how much inflection to give to their voices, which phrases to repeat, which questions to ask and when to pause so that the congregation can respond at the appropriate moment. Years of experience have made Pentecostal preachers some of the finest of all Latin American orators. They are superb communicators.

The preachers do all they can to identify with their people when they are on the platform. Their simple dress, their monosyllabic Spanish and their style of delivery are all designed for this purpose. In the Brazil for Christ Church, Manoel de Melo has even done away with a pulpit so that nothing will stand between him and his congregation. He paces back and forth on the huge platform, microphone in hand, while he preaches.

Pentecostal preachers have little difficulty in communicating spiritual truth in meaningful terms, well-suited to the particular level of understanding of their people. Their sermons may seem to a casual observer to be rather thin, but if so the standard of judgment might not reflect the preacher's own purpose. Pentecostal preaching is not intellectual, but emotional; it is not rational, but experiential; it is not exegetical, but allegorical; it is not doctrinal, but practical; it is not directed as much to the head as to the heart. The result of hearing Pentecostal preaching is not so much that you learn more, but rather that you feel better.

Some non-Pentecostals have sincerely been worried about this. They have felt that the lack of theological depth will endanger the whole church. I confess that for some time I, too, was concerned that the Pentecostals did not have as much theological sophistication as others of us would have liked. But, as Eugene Nida points out, we should beware of hasty judgments. He says, "A more careful analysis will often reveal something far more relevant than may have been thought at first."[7]

The themes of Pentecostal preaching, while not drawing on much church history, philosophy or systematic theology, do relate directly to where the people are living today. Pentecostal pastors are not bookish people who spend hours in the study preparing well-structured sermons. John Vaughan describes an interesting interview with one of Latin America's most effective preachers, Javier Vasquez of Chile's Jotabeche Methodist Pentecostal Church. Vasquez has two libraries, one at home and one in the church. "But," he says, "I don't have time to consult those books. I just stand by the Scripture which says, 'Take no thought beforehand what ye shall speak, neither do ye premeditate; but whatever shall be given you in that hour, that speak ye; for it is not ye that speak, but the Holy Ghost' (Mark 13:11). I go to the service completely empty; but confident that the Lord will give me the message for the service. So the Lord speaks through me in each service."[8]

Most Pentecostal pastors prefer to spend more time on the streets with the people than sermonizing. Thus, when they preach, they might not go as deeply into the text as their counterparts in more traditional churches, but they rarely miss the mark in meeting the felt needs of their listeners. A homiletics professor might not give them an "A" grade on the sermon, but the people will leave feeling blessed, spiritually nourished and motivated to serve God as well as possible for another week. In other words, their preaching has been successful.

These eight features of Pentecostal worship add up to a culturally relevant liturgy. Pentecostals have very positive feelings about what goes on in their church services, and consequently they bring others in with them. The main reason they have such positive feelings is, very simply, because it's fun to go to church.

Chapter Nine

Praying for the Sick

I cannot recall ever meeting an evangelical Christian who doubted God's ability to heal sickness without human medical aid. As a matter of fact, most of my friends have prayed for sick persons at one time or another, and some can testify to actual cases of healing. They are familiar with Jesus' healing ministry, with Peter and John's experience with the lame man at the gate called Beautiful, and with Paul's extraordinary healing of the sick on the island of Malta.

It is all the more curious, therefore, that some of these same evangelical Christians oppose the element of divine healing in Pentecostal churches. Next to speaking in tongues, divine healing seems to be the most severe point of tension between Pentecostals and non-Pentecostals in Latin America.

Embarrassed by the Pentecostals

I can say this with some authority, because not too

long ago I was one of the non-Pentecostals who militantly opposed divine healing campaigns. I clearly recall the visit of Puerto Rican faith healer Raimundo Jimenez to our city of Cochabamba, Bolivia. He came soon after a city-wide crusade held by an Argentine evangelist and sponsored by all the Protestant churches in the city, including the Pentecostals. With a great deal of effort and expense in publicity, visitation and physical arrangements, the Argentine was able to draw record-breaking crowds of slightly over 1,000 to the local basketball stadium.

A couple of weeks later the Pentecostals sponsored the second crusade on their own. The other, more traditional churches would not join them even though they had been invited. Since they didn't have money for a basketball stadium, they found a large vacant lot. Before the week was up they had crowds of 5,000 people who stood patiently throughout the entire service.

I must have suffered from a combination of incredulity, envy and perhaps just plain frustration at seeing those throngs of people gathering as a result of seemingly so little effort on the part of those who organized the crusade. With all our expertise, our crowds were peanuts in comparison. We, of course, warned people in our churches not to attend the Pentecostal crusade. We accused our rivals of sheep-stealing and false teaching (although we were hard-pressed when asked to explain just what their heresy was). But in spite of our counsel, virtually every member of our church attended some of the meetings. As if that weren't bad enough, some of them were healed!

I vented my frustrations in a nasty article, published in a nationally circulated Christian magazine. This brought down the wrath of many of my Pentecostal friends, and I was labeled as their public enemy number one for some time. Happily, I learned much from the Lord over the next few years, and the black mark beside my name has been largely erased. But having gone through these experiences, I can well understand the attitude of my non-Pentecostal brethren who are still where I was back in those days.

Dangers of Scoffing

At least I came out of the experience better than another non-Pentecostal scoffer in Mexico. One of the early leaders of the Apostolic Church of the Faith was Miguel Garcia, a tall, thin barber who had proved to be an effective evangelist and who founded the church in Torreon, among others.

When he first arrived in Torreon in 1918, Garcia was frequently invited to preach in the Methodist, Baptist and Presbyterian churches there. Soon afterward, however, the invitations abruptly ceased. He learned that the pastors were opposed to his teaching on two points: speaking in tongues and divine healing. So Garcia started his own meetings.

One wealthy and prominent evangelical decided to challenge Garcia publicly. Every day at about the same time a paralyzed man would drag himself past the rich man's home. The rich man stopped him and asked him where he was going. "To Garcia's meetings," he answered. "I want to be healed."

The rich man poked fun at him and told him he was wasting his time. "I'll lose my neck before I ever see you healed," he said with a sneer. Just a few days later, however, the paralyzed man was walking normally. And the rich man? He died suddenly with an infection in his neck! Understandably, the outward opposition to Garcia came to an abrupt halt.[1]

The moment of truth is almost unavoidable for non-Pentecostals in Latin America. With 80 percent of evangelicals calling themselves Pentecostals, and with the percentage rising every year, what Pentecostals do there cannot be ignored. It will not help to pretend the problem doesn't exist. When needy men and women can find something in other churches that yours does not offer, when this is something good, and when it has biblical support, a great deal of honesty and open-mindedness is called for. Non-Pentecostals in Latin America would be well-advised to anticipate the coming moment of truth rather than let it take them by surprise.

In Guayaquil, Ecuador, the reality of divine healing took many Christians by surprise. I told the story of the highly successful Foursquare crusade in Guayaquil, Ecuador, in Chapters 3 and 4. But I have not yet mentioned one additional factor that contributed heavily to its success: Divine healing was one of the keys to baptizing 1,500 new Christians and planting seven new churches in six weeks.

The Foursquare missionary, Roberto Aguirre, had been led to believe by the other pastors in the city that they would cooperate in his crusade just as Aguirre had cooperated with theirs a few months previously. Then, as the date approached, the other pastors quietly began to back off. They had heard that the evangelist who was coming from California was Roberto Espinoza, a faith healer. A meeting was called after Espinoza arrived, and not a single one of the other pastors showed up. The Foursquare leaders were sad and rather nervous. They had already paid $1,000 for the stadium and $1,000 for the expenses of Espinoza and his wife. Since they could no longer depend on their skeptical colleagues, they were forced to cast themselves entirely upon God.

God did not let them down. The very day before the meetings were to begin, the owner of a large radio station came to see Aguirre. Aguirre had never met the man and assumed he was coming for business reasons—to sell radio time. But the budget had already been overspent, and barely any advertising at all had been done for the crusade. Aguirre wondered how the radio man even knew there were going to be meetings in Guayaquil.

The man was remarkably cordial, however, and said that he would like to offer his radio station to broadcast the services. "I'm sorry," Aguirre said, "but we have no money."

"Money is no problem," the radio man answered. "I have come to offer my radio time free. If you pay the expenses of the technician, you can have it."

It goes without saying that Aguirre could hardly believe his ears. Then he probed to find out what God had done to motivate the radio station owner. Lo and behold, Aguirre discovered that the man had recently been healed through the prayers of a member of Aguirre's congregation! He was so grateful for renewed health that he wanted as many others as possible in Guayaquil to have it as well.

The first night the crowd was disappointing. Fewer than 1,000 persons showed up. But Roberto Espinoza prayed for the sick that night and four deaf people and 12 others with hernias were healed. The whole thing was broadcast to Guayaquil over the radio, and the news spread rapidly. Attendance the second night rose to 10,000; it was up to 20,000 by the end of the first week; and before the crusade ended, the number of people standing in the vast open field was estimated at between 35,000 and 40,000. Many dramatic healings took place, but more important, "The Lord added to the church daily such as should be saved," in this case 1,500 in six weeks.[2]

Healing Is Widespread

Studies have shown that faith healing is a more universal characteristic of Latin American Pentecostals than other charismatic gifts, for example, speaking in tongues. In a survey of Pentecostal pastors in Chile, Lalive found that whereas only 57 percent of them had spoken in tongues, a full 98 percent had been instruments for divine healing.[3] It is necessary, therefore, to understand the role of praying for the sick if one is to uncover the dynamics of Pentecostalism in Latin America.

As we have pointed out many times, the Pentecostal message seems particularly relevant to the working lower classes of Latin America. These same lower classes have a saying that goes, *"Enfermarse es un lujo"*—getting sick is a luxury. In many of the rural villages of Latin America medical aid is nonexistent, and in the cities few can squeeze the costs of medical and hospital bills out of their skimpy budgets. The use of folk medicine is very common, and while it is at times remarkably helpful this is not always the case. Many go beyond folk medicine to witchcraft, and it is painful to admit that some born-again Christians, perhaps more than we would want to think, turn to witch doctors because they do not know where else to go in their desperation.

In Mexico, a young Otomi Indian man, Ausencio Gonzalez, has become one of the most aggressive church planters in the area. Making the initial contacts through

Bible distribution and street preaching, he has multiplied churches in remote rural areas as well as in Mexico City. In 1982 he had originated 25 groups, and within two years they had increased to 400. Part of his preaching is an uncomplicated belief that God heals today with the same power described in the New Testament.

In Mexico City the parents of a 12-year-old boy asked Ausencio Gonzalez to go with them to the hospital to pray for their child. He was paralyzed, deaf and dumb. When they got to the hospital the staff would not allow them to pray the way many Pentecostals do because they would disturb the other patients. So Ausencio said, "Let's take him outside." They put him in a wheelchair and went out, stopping at the busy exit of the subway station. A crowd gathered. Gonzalez announced publicly that God was going to heal the boy even though the doctors in the hospital could not do anything and they had said there was no hope for him to get well. When they finished the prayer, Ausencio said, "Stand up." The father made signs because he was deaf. He stood up and got out of the wheel chair!

He couldn't talk and tell them how he felt, so Ausencio prayed and asked God to remove the deafness and dumbness. He said, "Mama" and "Papa," and then they taught him to sing a chorus, *"Cristo viene muy pronto."*

Many in the crowd at the subway exit received Christ as Lord and Savior on the spot. Several of them then ran into the hospital and brought out sick friends and relatives. One 36-year-old man had a severe heart disease. The doctors had told him that he needed an operation but probably would die anyway. The group prayed for him, and first he accepted Christ into his life. Then Gonzalez said, "Repeat this prayer after me," and he shouted the prayer right there in the street. The sick man shouted with him. "Is there any more pain?" Ausencio asked. "No," he said, "I'm healed!" "Let's test it," Ausencio suggested. "Run over there to that sign and back." He did, with no ill effects. The crowd began to cheer and many more came to Christ.[4]

When common people like this hear that faith in God alone can produce healing without electrocardiograms, prescriptions, injections or even fetishes, it is no wonder they are attracted. The physical suffering that is so much a part of today's Latin America becomes a strong motivating force to bring men and women under the hearing of the message the Pentecostals preach.

The Priority of Salvation

No one should assume that, because of this, physical healing has become more important in Pentecostal preaching than spiritual salvation. This brings up the matter of priorities, a point which non-Pentecostals often raise. They tend to say, "They may preach some spectacular kind of bodily healing, but we preach Christ and Him crucified as salvation from sin." This creates a dichotomy which may be helpful for polemical purposes, but which Pentecostals do not feel. There is no question in the minds of any Pentecostals I know that the eternal dimension of the salvation of the soul is a higher priority than the temporal dimension of the healing of the body. But to them it is not an either/or, but a both/and situation.

When Read, Monterroso and Johnson wrote *Latin American Church Growth* they were concerned with this problem. During their field research they often probed deeply to discover what were true Pentecostal priorities. They found that a rather consistent thread of faith healing ran through the most successful of the evangelistic crusades, such as those held by Tommy Hicks in Argentina, A. A. Allen in Venezuela, and Morris Cerullo in Uruguay. But they make a point of adding that "in all these campaigns, the principal element is the preaching of the gospel. Healing is presented as just one of the blessings that God provided in Christ and His saving work."[5]

To illustrate, a Chilean pastor tells of a family that brought their mother to him with a paralyzed leg. They sought him out because he had a small truck, and they asked him to take her to the hospital. The truck was broken and would require several hours to fix. So the pastor said, "Listen, I will gladly take you to the hospital, but it will take time to fix the truck. But I also know that we, the Pentecostals, can cure your mother."

They wanted nothing to do with Pentecostals; they simply wanted transportation so they could get competent medical help. The pastor then made the following proposition: "We will fix the truck, but while we are doing it, the brothers will come and pray. If, by the time we are ready to go, your mother is cured, will you agree to be converted to the Lord?"

They reluctantly agreed. When the truck was fixed and ready to go, the Christians picked up the mother they had been praying for, and she moved her leg. The paralysis was gone. She had been cured. From that time on the whole family began coming to the Pentecostal services.[6]

Healing Attracts Attention

This typical story shows that Pentecostals are interested in the ultimate effect that divine healing will have on eternal salvation. Among Pentecostals in Colombia, Donald Palmer found that the consistent attitude toward faith healing is similar to how one Pentecostal pastor put it: "The object of healing for the unsaved is as bait. It attracts their attention to the power of Christ, who can also save."[7] Healing, although a good thing, is not considered an end in itself by most Latin American Pentecostals. It is for the most part a manifestation of the power of God that will ultimately attract unbelievers to Jesus Christ as Savior and Lord. Healing is, thus, an effective evangelistic tool which only incidentally brings temporal blessings.

Some Pentecostals go to unfortunate extremes. Manuel Gaxiola tells of some early trends in Mexico that declared the use of any kind of medicine, including aspirin and Mentholatum, to be conclusive evidence of lack of faith, and consequently grounds for excommunication.[8] Palmer found that in Colombia, while the United Pentecostals would permit Alka-Seltzer and vitamins, they strictly prohibited the use of doctors or strong medicines in the past.

This attitude is changing in Colombia, however.[9] It is not typical of Latin American Pentecostals in general. Most Pentecostals do not prohibit the use of modern medicine. If doctors are available and money is on hand to pay the bills, ordinary healing processes are encouraged, although always accompanied by prayer. But when medical help is not available for one reason or another, the gift of healing is brought into play.

Miracles and Healing

Some Pentecostals make a fine distinction between the gift of healing and the gift of miracles. Healing is the supernatural intervention of the power of God in cases that apparently could also be cured by doctors in hospitals, if the patients could afford them. Miracles, on the other hand, involve cases that have deteriorated beyond the possibilities of medical science. A virus infection or an abscess or dysentery are cared for by the gift of healing. Cancer or congenital mental retardation need the gift of miracles. Both are present among Latin American Pentecostals, but healing is much more common than miracles.

The most publicized cases of divine healing are usually those that fall into the category of miracles. A little boy who was healed in the great Tommy Hicks crusade in Buenos Aires in 1954 received city-wide press coverage, and this in turn drew multitudes to the meetings. Some considered it the turning point of the crusade. It just so happened that when the mother brought this 3-year-old boy with a brace on his deformed leg, four physicians were on the platform. After prayer, the brace was removed and in plain sight of thousands of people the boy walked, then ran, then jumped. The people began to cheer. Then one of the physicians moved over to the boy. The mother looked up at him. Incredibly, he was the very same doctor who had fitted the brace and told her that the boy would need it for the rest of his life!

The emotion of the moment was so high that both the mother and the doctor began to weep profusely. Then when he examined the leg, he dropped to his knees and said, "I want this Christ. I want to be saved." According to Hicks, this doctor and also one of his colleagues accepted Christ that night.[10] Hicks was thankful for the healing, but typically, even more so that the healing had brought these two men into eternal salvation.

Healing in the Churches

Divine healing in crusades such as Hicks, Espinoza and Jimenez conducted is sporadic. The crusades come and go, but the churches stay on. How then do the churches pray for the sick on a more regular basis?

A good bit of the day-by-day healing happens in the sick rooms. Pentecostals in Latin America take quite literally the verse in James that says, "Is anyone among you sick? Let him call for the elders of the church, and let them pray over him, anointing him with oil in the name of the Lord; and the prayer offered in faith will restore the one who is sick" (James 5:14-15). I wouldn't be surprised if some Pentecostals pray for the sick as often as Presbyterians repeat the Lord's Prayer. And they continue to believe in it because they all have seen it work so frequently.

The liturgy in many Pentecostal churches includes faith healing as a matter of routine. In the Jotabeche Church in Chile healing occurs after the main service. The pastor remains in the front of the sanctuary, and a line forms by the platform. Some persons simply want to greet the pastor, some have brought him a gift, and others ask him to pray for a personal problem or for healing. When the prayer involves healing, the believer will kneel, and the pastor will place his hands upon the head.

Much more prominent as a part of the liturgy is the healing service in the Brazil for Christ Church in Sao Paulo. There, when the proper point in the liturgy arrives, Pastor Manoel de Melo ceremoniously removes his suit jacket and puts on a double-breasted white coat. He then announces what particular sickness he will deal with. He might be treating head problems that night, for example. If so, he will go into a lengthy description of every conceivable physical malady that can occur from one of these problems and will ask those who suffer from them to come forward. Out of the congregation of up to 10,000, hundreds will respond until the space in front of the platform is filled.

The treatment begins with an explanation of the medical importance of the head, followed by a brief sermon on divine healing. This is designed to build up weak faith to the point where it may be exercised effectively. When this is over, de Melo has the entire congregation stand.

"Does the church believe that Jesus can heal?" he asks.

"Yes, the church believes that Jesus can heal!" comes the response from thousands of people.

He repeats it several times, until it sounds like the waves of the ocean breaking over rocks. Then he leads in the prayer of faith for the sick and moves out among the sick people, touching their heads and praying for them one by one. He concludes by having the congregation repeat after him the final prayer, with hands uplifted.

Edward Murphy, who has done special research on the Brazil for Christ Church, was present at one service where de Melo dismissed all the sick people but one. He took one elderly man up on the platform with him and said, "I kept this man here on purpose. He has a serious problem. He is blind. This sickness is of the devil. When I put my hand on him, I felt heat in my hand. I know the Lord Jesus is curing him right this instant. He is now being healed."

The congregation broke out into applause, and the man sat down. Then, to heighten the drama, de Melo called the man back and said, "He was healed. Now he can see," and he had the man follow him back and forth across the platform.

By that time, Murphy says, "the people went almost hysterical with joy, clapping, raising their hands to Jesus, and praising Him for His healing power."[11]

Dealing With Demons

Notice that de Melo said, "This is of the devil." That brings up one more point that needs to be mentioned in a chapter on faith healing, namely exorcism. Demonic power is not recognized and dealt with in many of the slower growing non-Pentecostal churches in Latin America, but it is a frequent subject of sermon, discussion and action in the Pentecostal churches.

So far as I have been able to determine, the only detailed analysis of this aspect of Latin American Pentecostalism was done by missionary Harmon Johnson in a work entitled *Authority Over the Spirits: Brazilian Spiritism and Evangelical Church Growth.*[12] Johnson enviably combines the objectivity of a scholar, the personal involvement of a Pentecostal (Assemblies of God), and many years of firsthand experience in Brazil in this definitive study.

By choosing Brazil, Johnson has moved into the territory where the power of the devil may be more directly and universally felt than in any other Latin American country with the exception of Haiti. While all Brazilians are not spiritists, virtually all of their lives have been touched at one point or another by this religion of the devil. Johnson's conclusions, therefore, can be applied much further afield than just to Brazil.

Although written with great sensitivity, one of Johnson's findings amounts to a severe rebuke for non-Pentecostals. The most typical reaction of non-Pentecostals to spiritism has been one of polemics, and the kind of polemics which indicates that they do not take the validity of spiritism very seriously. "It is difficult to see," Johnson says, "how any spiritist would be interested in reading through any book which concentrates on the negative aspects of spiritism, and which talks mostly about fraud, superstition, credulity, and the triviality of a religion to which he has committed his whole life."[13]

It is no wonder that non-Pentecostal churches are winning so few people from spiritism in Brazil, relatively speaking. Spiritism is not simply ignorance, superstition and chicanery. A Christianity which does not recognize it as a manifestation of the powers of darkness will continue to be impotent in this particular field of evangelism.

The Power Encounter

The Pentecostal churches in Brazil go to the heart of the matter and recognize spiritism for what it is—supernatural, demonic activity. They believe that the miracles worked by spirits are real, but that they can be traced to Satan. Consequently, their evangelistic approach to spiritists stresses the power encounter, and they are not afraid to pit the power of God against the power of Satan any more than Elijah was when he faced the priests of Baal on Mt. Carmel. Their message is that of "Christ the Victor," and a common theme in preaching is deliverance from the powers of Satan. This is the kind of message that spiritists understand and respond to.

The experience of Giberto Stevao, a leader of Umbanda spiritism before his conversion, is considered by Johnson to be typical. Stevao was converted; he had received the Pentecostal experience, but it took 12 additional days for him to face his power encounter. He had gone to bed, read his New Testament and turned out the light. But he could not sleep. The wind whistling through the bushes outside produced a great fear in him until he was seized with chills. He was paralyzed with fear. He knew a demon, a "spirit of rebellion," had entered his room. Then he heard a nearby voice saying, "Chi-chi-chi."

Stevao says, "I cried in my heart, 'What shall I do, Jesus?' But it appeared to me that He was far away...I began to cry. 'The blood of Jesus has power. I rebuke you, Satan. I cast you out by the blood of Jesus.' But it seemed like I was saying vain words. No result."

The encounter continued, unabated, throughout the night. Stevao's soul had become the battleground for a ferociously spiritual struggle. But as time went by, courage and faith began to build up. Finally, Stevao dared to cry out, "Satan, you lying enemy! I am and always will be a friend and companion of the Lord Jesus Christ! Go, and may the blood of Jesus Christ crush your head!" With that, the demon left, and Stevao had been liberated.[14]

Without building the power encounter into your doctrine and practice, you cannot be effective in reaching the millions of Latin Americans who are subject to demonic activity of one kind or another. Exorcism of demons is a part of the ministry of almost all Latin American Pentecostal churches, and Johnson feels that, at least in Brazil, it is the most important key to Pentecostal church growth.[15]

In Chapter 2 I described how Omar Cabrera of Santa Fe, Argentina, engages in spiritual warfare with the powers of the air before each major crusade. This is ministry in the power encounter on a high level, for if the dominion of the forces of evil can be broken over a geographic territory, prayer for the sick can be that much more effective. Extraordinary miracles take place through Cabrera's ministry on a regular basis. For example, in one meeting a woman came toward him carrying a small child whose head was wrapped in a bandana. God let Cabrera know that something unusual was going to happen by giving him a sort of electrical feeling in his upper body. Since then Cabrera has learned to recognize it as the creative power of God preparing to manifest, but this was the first time. The mother explained that the child had been born without ears. In the name of Jesus, Cabrera commanded the ears to grow and then told the mother to remove the bandana. By the time it was off, two small pink buds had begun to come out on the sides of the head. Then with a snap like bubble gum, both ears burst out in the plain view of many people who were observing.

This event was a sign of the coming of the kingdom of God, just as similar events of healing and liberation are worldwide. Each one brings embarrassment to the devil and glory to God. That is why with stories of supernatural signs and wonders come encouraging stories of multitudes coming to Christ. Power evangelism is becoming more widely known day by day.

Some non-Pentecostal churches, happily, are listening. Many more need to if they are to increase their effectiveness. Praying for the sick and casting out demons are New Testament practices which should not hastily be pushed outside the sphere of Christian experience. The influence of secularism and scientism has dulled the edge of Christian sensitivity to these matters, undoubtedly to Satan's advantage. We can be thankful that Pentecostals in Latin America, among others, are reminding us that, in the 20th century as well as in the first, we can preach a gospel of power, and that Christ is Liberator.

Chapter Ten

In Non-Pentecostal Churches

The Latin American Congress on Evangelization, held in Bogota in 1969, was the largest and most spectacular gathering of Latin American evangelical leaders up to that time. Over 900 delegates from every Latin American republic except Cuba met to develop strategies to increase evangelistic fervor and effectiveness over the whole continent.

At the Bogota Congress, Latin American evangelicals for the first time became aware of a new and highly significant development within Protestant churches. Ruben Lores, then president of the Latin American Biblical Seminary of San Jose, Costa Rica, stirred the delegates with an address in which he described the entrance of Pentecostal practices into some non-Pentecostal churches. Many delegates congratulated Lores for his courage in dealing on such a high level with an obviously controversial topic. Others, predictably, expressed strong displeasure at the message. Events since 1969, however, have shown how prophetic Lores' address really was.

Lores called the charismatic movement in Latin America a fulfillment of Joel's prophecy as quoted by Peter on Pentecost:

And it shall be in the last days, God says, That I will pour forth of My Spirit upon all mankind; And your sons and your daughters shall prophesy, And your young men shall see visions, And your old men shall dream dreams....

Lores traced the history of the charismatic movement in the United States over recent decades through three streams: classical Pentecostals, "Penteprotestants" and "Pentecatholics." He described the renewing power of these charismatic manifestations in the churches in dramatically optimistic terms. Then he said that churches in Puerto Rico, Guatemala, Costa Rica, Colombia, Chile, Argentina and Brazil had also been renewed through the charismatic movement.[1]

This brought it close to home for the delegates. Too close for some. Since then, one of the questions foremost in the minds of Latin American evangelicals has been: To what extent has the Pentecostal movement spilled over the boundaries of the Pentecostal denominations and entered the more traditional churches? I will attempt to answer that with the data we have. I will also zero in on the questions more directly related to this book. What *effect* has this had on the non-Pentecostal churches where Pentecostal practices have entered? Has this, in fact, helped churches to grow?

Victor Landero's Spontaneous Combustion

During the 1950s the Roman Catholic persecution of the Protestants in Colombia was so fierce that it became one of the notorious examples of violation of human rights in our day. Hundreds of Protestants were brutally murdered for their faith. Many others of them fled into the uninhabited parts of Colombia in order to conserve both their faith and their lives. One of these, deep in the forest region of northern Colombia, would ride out on horseback to preach and sell Bibles in the small, backwoods towns.

He couldn't have suspected it at the time, but one of the Bibles he sold eventually sparked what has been called a "spontaneous combustion" movement to Christ. A local bartender, Victor Landero,[2] who also managed a house of prostitutes, bought the Bible, read it and was converted in 1957. He dismissed his prostitutes, sold his bar and worked on his small farm for a while. Then he bought a new farm upriver in order to enter an unevangelized area. Many of his new neighbors were converted. He was so excited that he asked God to help him feed his family so he could give more time to Christian work. Eventually only two days a week were required to keep the farm producing. The other five were God's, and they were used in effective evangelism.

There were no missionaries or other Colombian Christians directing this movement. God here had the opportunity to instruct these new believers with only the Bible and the Holy Spirit. He did it in ways more reminiscent of the book of Acts than perhaps of the typical contemporary missionary handbook.

One night Victor Landero had a vivid dream of a certain hut in the woods, which he had never seen before.[3] A clear voice said to him, "The people in that hut are dying without Christ because no one ever told them of Him." It took some time to do it, but months later Victor started out through the woods with no idea where he was going. After only two days, he came into a clearing and saw the hut of which he had dreamed. He knocked on the door, met the family and told them why he had come.

The woman of the house was speechless. Only three nights previously, she had dreamed a strange dream. She saw her house full of people with a stranger talking to them out of a book. The word "gospel" came to her in her dream, although she had never heard the word before.

News spread, and that evening 24 neighbors came to hear the stranger talk out of the book. Every one of them received Christ. The next night 10 more came, and they, too, were converted. All of them later continued in the apostles' doctrine, fellowship, breaking of bread and prayers, just as they did in the book of Acts. Landero went home rejoicing.

The Prayer Meeting in the Forest

Soon a seeming obstacle appeared on the horizon. A false cult had begun moving through the area in 1961, preaching heretical doctrine. Victor Landero became so disturbed at his inability to refute these errors intellectually that he began to take frequent trips to a secluded place in the forest to fast and pray. He spent many hours there crying bitterly before God. Some other believers joined him. One day something unusual happened. They were overcome with a sense of joy that they could not explain. They prayed through the night and read the book of Acts to each other. After they had done this several times, spontaneously one of them spoke in tongues! Others soon began to do the same.

A type of charismatic movement had started in the Colombia forest, but it was a "spontaneous combustion'' process. Obviously, this particular manifestation of the Spirit had come down from heaven. It was not something that had been taught to them by other Christians.

This happened here not *because of*, but *in spite of*, the missionaries. By this time, American missionaries from a non-Pentecostal mission had discovered the group and were encouraging it from time to time. But their first reaction to the outbreak of this charismatic movement was not favorable. They found themselves in a dilemma. The mission had a policy of allowing the local leadership to direct the work, and in this case the local leadership was leading the charismatic movement. They decided that the best approach would be to have a series of Bible studies on the Holy Spirit with the believers.

The Bible studies were designed to point out Pentecostal errors indirectly, without mentioning Pentecostalism at all. The effect was just the opposite, however. As one of the Colombian leaders expresses it, the Bible studies were just like throwing gasoline on the fire. Not only did the local believers gain more confidence in using the gifts they had been given, but the news of these gifts began to spread to other churches in the area.

Soon after the gift of tongues came the gift of interpretation. One of the first messages received through tongues and interpretation was a clear command to persevere in what they were doing. They received it as the voice of God. Then they started praying for the sick, and many were healed. A blind man received his sight. A paralytic began to walk for the first time. Young men saw visions, and old men dreamed dreams. Everyone was praising the Lord. Worries about the false cult evaporated when the Spirit began to show His power.

God gave some the gift of prophecy. A girl was having serious personal problems, but none of her friends was able to get her to admit them and confess her sin. At a regional Bible conference, however, a young fellow who did not know the girl received a prophecy from God. He stood up in a public meeting and said, "Is Senorita so-and-so here?" Her heart came up in her throat! He named her problems specifically and then gave her instructions from God as to how to deal with them. She fell to her knees in repentance, and the matter was cared for instantly. She was liberated, the others were blessed, and the gift of prophecy had edified the body.

The Fetish Turns to Powder

Witchcraft is common back in the Colombian forests, and the power of God is needed to deal with it. As in the case of Brazil, the power encounter between Jesus and the devil is taken very seriously. Manuel Sena, for example, had been a sorcerer before his conversion. Secretly he wrapped one of his metal fetishes in a cloth, hid it inside a jar and put the jar in a storage box. Although a Christian, the demons would not let him alone after that. In desperation, he finally asked his brothers to help him, and they prayed for him one night. He was thrown to the ground by some demonic power, and while in a coma a strange voice came out of his mouth telling the others about the fetish. Sena later confessed that it was true.

The next day Victor Landero went home with him. His wife had also gone through a terrifying demonic experience the night before. She had felt a horrible fear of the box where the fetish was hidden. She had prayed, and as she did, their dog had started barking and rushing around the room as if someone were chasing him. Finally things calmed down enough, and she slept the rest of the night.

Landero listened to her story, then with a quickened pulse took the jar out of the box and opened it. Lo and behold! The metal fetish had completely disintegrated and turned to grey powder! From that moment on, Manuel Sena was liberated from the demons.[4]

Social Service and Church Growth

One of the products of this spontaneous combustion movement has been a remarkably well-organized and effective program of grassroots social service, organized by Victor Landero's younger brother, Gregorio. It is not some imported program, but springs from local initiative. Through their organization called *Accion Unida*, new industries have been established, farmers have begun to produce for the commercial market as well as just for their families, epidemics have been stayed, savings and loan agencies have been set up, people are learning to read and write, and new prosperity has begun to cover the area, benefiting both believers and unbelievers.[5]

But the church grew. In 1960 this group of Christians met in 10 organized churches and 15 newer congregations. Ten years later they numbered 47 churches and 86 congregations. They are all actively planting daughter churches. The larger churches run to 300 members. The annual rate of growth has run a healthy 15 percent to 20 percent. To keep pace with such rapid growth, leadership patterns needed to change also. In 1960 the churches had 12 pastors, all trained in traditional seminaries. A decade after, only two seminary-trained pastors remained. The work was carried on by 60 other fully supported workers plus 64 additional workers who earn their own living.

One of the interesting things about these churches is that they dislike the word "Pentecostal." They strongly object if anyone refers to them as Pentecostal churches. They prefer "renewal." They are affiliated with the Association of Evangelical Churches of the Caribbean, a non-Pentecostal denomination which grew out of the Latin America Mission. As non-Pentecostal churches, however, they act like Pentecostals, they look a great deal like Pentecostals, and more important they also *grow* like Pentecostals. If they will pardon my saying it, here, by spontaneous combustion, the Pentecostal movement has entered non-Pentecostal churches. Call it what you may, the brothers and sisters there are delighted at the way the Holy Spirit is using them in their area.

Opposing the Pentecostals

If you asked the leader of almost any non-Pentecostal church (or of some decadent Pentecostal churches as well), "Wouldn't you like the Lord to use you as He is using Victor Landero and the others in Colombia?," the response would almost invariably be "Yes." Most Christians covet that kind of joy, enthusiasm and effectiveness in reaching their community. But despite this honest desire, many evangelicals still oppose "Pentecostalizing tendencies."

This is not new. It happened back in the days of Willis Hoover in Chile. After the Methodist Pentecostal Church split off from them, the Methodists who remained reacted so strongly that they even stopped saying "Amen" in their services. They discontinued personal evangelism, open-air preaching and prayer meetings just so they wouldn't look very much like Pentecostals. The Methodist missionaries also failed to see that the new Pentecostal movement was something authentically Chilean, not merely an extension of Hoover's views. Deep down, the Chileans in the Methodist Pentecostal Church blamed the missionaries for the stifling of the Holy Spirit's activity in their former church.[6]

In his message to the Congress on Evangelization, Ruben Lores inferred as much. "We see all over," he said, "a growing sense of impatience with the foreign missions and with the ecclesiastical structures they have created." He pled for new freedom in all of the churches for the Holy Spirit to act as He will. "Are we by some stretch of the imagination agencies of a commercial enterprise directed from New York or Geneva?" he asked the delegates. "Let us allow the Holy Spirit to be truly Lord," he concluded, "because the Lord is that Spirit; and where the Spirit of the Lord is, there is liberty."[7]

It is bad enough for non-Pentecostals to ignore what the Spirit is doing through Pentecostal brethren. This becomes even worse, however, when some actively and officially oppose such movings of God. This opposition frequently is couched in doctrinal terminology. I have a copy of an official denominational policy statement before me which illustrates how this can go to an extreme. I will not reveal the source, except to point out that the denomination was founded by an evangelical mission and that foreign missionary influence in the national church is still considerable, although not total. In this particular country, the renewal movement in non-Pentecostal churches has been strong, provoking such a policy formulation. Here is a portion of the document, literally translated from the Spanish:

"Recently some non-Pentecostal groups have arisen which attempt to bring into their meetings such

Pentecostal customs and practices as clapping while singing, worldly music, and the excessive use of sacred expressions like hallelujahs and amens with no thought as to the meaning of such expressions...We believe that the current fad of speaking in tongues is not regulated by Holy Scripture...We advise those brethren in our own churches who have Pentecostal tendencies to seek their fellowship somewhere else rather than try to change our long-standing tradition...."

Fortunately this negative attitude on the part of some non-Pentecostals seems to be diminishing as we move through the '80s. God is using many means to bring about a change from the negative to the positive. One of His instruments for doing this was David Howard who in the '60s was the Colombia field director for the Latin America Mission. He was the first missionary to come into contact with Victor Landero and the movement which had sprung up through his ministry. The easiest and safest thing to do would have been for David Howard to reject the movement as a false sect. But he took a more positive approach.

Howard, who is now executive secretary of the World Evangelical Fellowship, had no Pentecostal inclinations himself. But he said that when he found charismatic manifestations among the believers in the Colombia forest, he felt like Peter did when God lowered the great sheet full of unclean animals in Acts 10. God spoke to him as he did to Peter. He told Peter to accept the Gentiles. He told David Howard to accept the charismatic brothers and sisters. Howard testifies that "slowly, God removed our skepticism, confirming the gifts of the Spirit by showing the fruit of the Spirit in the lives of the believers who receive these gifts...They showed more love, joy, peace, and other Christian attributes than many Christians who have known the Lord for years."[8] Howard and his colleagues exercised Christian patience and tolerance in what was for them an unusual and difficult situation. They have never regretted it, for the Spirit of God has continued to work in many extraordinary ways, and most of all, the Lord is adding *daily* to the church such as should be saved.

Out to the Streets

Perhaps one reason why I am convinced that non-Pentecostal churches can learn much from the Pentecostals in Latin America is that our own church did. My family and I belonged to one of the largest churches in the city of Cochabamba, Bolivia, called the Calle Bolivar Church. It was situated only one-half block from the plaza in the middle of the city. It had an excellent location, but it had become very routine and nominal. The pastor was deeply concerned. He wanted to win people to Christ and plant new churches. But the inertia was almost overwhelming. The denomination, the *Union Cristiana Evangelica*, had four churches in Cochabamba in 1964, and in 1969 there were still four. The city was growing, but the church wasn't. Members seemed to attend church from force of habit. Wide yawns, mentioned previously, were commonplace. Few had much desire to bring their non-Christian friends to church, because it just wasn't much fun. Decisions for Christ were rare, and baptisms took place perhaps once or twice a year.

Then a Pentecostal pastor from Chile passed through town. The pastor of our church met him and learned of some of the things the Spirit of God was doing in Chile. He became so enthusiastic that he invited the Chilean to take his Sunday morning pulpit. Sunday morning sermons there were ordinarily 20 minutes long, but the Chilean held the congregation spellbound for a full hour. Among other things, he said, "I'll bet you people have been praying that the Lord would bring unbelievers into your church to be saved." He paused. Scores nodded their heads. Then he let a bomb fall. He frowned, pointed his finger and said, "But that prayer of yours is a sin! You have been disobedient! You know very well that the Lord has commanded you to 'go and preach the gospel to all creatures.' Then you turn around and pray that He will bring them in without your going. God will not bless you unless you *go out* and take the gospel to the people where they are!"

That was just what the church needed. The very next Sunday the church began going out, and up until we left Bolivia six months later it had continued. On the average Sunday night, 30 to 40 believers would gather at the church door an hour before the service. Some would bring accordions, some guitars, some drums and other instruments. Two or three would come with open pick-up trucks. The pastor would form groups and send them out into the streets.

The open-air meetings drew good crowds around the marketplace. When they were over, the leaders would invite the onlookers to climb into the trucks and come to church with them. Full truckloads of people would pull up to the church doors, and then the musicians would all congregate on the street in front of the church for the final meeting. Traffic would slow to a crawl. Invariably passers-by would come into the church. Then the musicians would all go up front and form an orchestra of sorts for the meeting. With a full church and lively music, it became fun to go to church once again.

As a result, people began coming to Christ. From the time we began going out to the people and "Pentecostalizing'' our service slightly, until the time we left Bolivia, not a Sunday night went by without from 1 to 27 decisions for Christ. Baptisms were being held once a month instead of once a year. New congregations were being formed in several other places in the city. Although no charismatic manifestations were evident in this non-Pentecostal church, it did learn much from its Pentecostal brethren about how churches grow.

Renewal in Templo Biblico

The Templo Biblico of San Jose, Costa Rica, was another church located in the middle of a capital city, but it had become dull and stagnant. I visited it once in 1963 and again 10 years later in 1972. In 1962 I saw a healthy, growing church, but nothing spectacular. In 1972, however, I could hardly believe my eyes. When I went to the Sunday morning service I had a difficult time finding a seat. Standing room only had become the norm. When the service started and people prayed with their hands lifted up, I had an inkling of what might have happened. Later I found out for sure.[9]

The church had taken a spiritual nosedive in the period 1967-1970. By 1970 attendance had dropped from 600 to 200 on Sunday morning and from 400 to about 40 on Sunday night. Pessimism and depression had gripped the leaders. Personal problems plagued the choir, the Sunday school teachers, and even the board of elders. In desperation the trustees even grappled with the consideration of selling the property. They were ready to abandon the church and each go their own way. They prayed weakly that God would do something and they themselves did as much as they could. They invited Alberto Mottesi, one of the Baptist pastors deeply involved in the renewal movement in Argentina, to minister to them. They invited others from time to time. Each of these servants of God contributed to the coming renewal movement, but the dramatic breakthrough had not yet occurred.

Then the Lord sent someone they had not invited. He was Francis MacNutt from Notre Dame, an American priest who had become associated with the Catholic charismatic movement in the United States. Few people at the Templo Biblico had even heard of him until the news began to spread that he had come to Costa Rica to preach renewal to the Catholics there. Some evangelical leaders of the renewal movement, among them Ruben Lores, however, had been informed of the development of these plans from the beginning.[10]

The pastor and some of the elders of the Templo Biblico went to hear him in a private home, by special invitation. It was a small meeting, with only a few present. MacNutt and a registered nurse, Mrs. Barbara Shlemon, gave their testimonies of renewal. Afterwards all was quiet for a time. An invitation to pray for the fullness of the Spirit was given. Someone started crying and then began laughing uncontrollably. Several others had a similar experience. The atmosphere was electric, and the presence of the Holy Spirit was evident. Impressed, the Protestants invited MacNutt to speak at the Templo Biblico that next Sunday night.

They advertised the meeting on the radio. The very novelty of having a Catholic priest in a Protestant service for the first time was enough to arouse curiosity and an overflow crowd packed into the large building. Again, the priest and Mrs. Schlemon repeated their simple testimonies. Then things began to happen that had never before happened in the Templo Biblico. The structured service was over, but spontaneously people began going up front to pray, and MacNutt laid his hands on some as he felt led. Some were singing, some were laughing, some began speaking in tongues and some even singing in tongues.

Needless to say, the Templo Biblico took a new lease on life. At least a dozen were coming to Christ every Sunday, sometimes many more. Remarkable conversions became the order of the day. The church was full Sunday morning and Sunday night. The attitude of the believers changed. They invited their friends because it was so much fun to go to church. Baptisms became frequent, with between 25 and 125 at each baptism. Sometimes the elders took turns baptizing because there were so many candidates. And new churches started up in other parts of the city.

Now, after all of that, the Templo Biblico did not consider itself a Pentecostal church. It is a Bible church in the evangelical tradition. It has not split off from any other group, nor does it plan to. The Association of Bible Churches which it belongs to, although a non-Pentecostal denomination, is not bringing charges of one sort or another against the Templo Biblico. Just the opposite. The experience of revival began to spread through sister churches in Costa Rica.

What Can We Learn?

An important question raised by many sincere Latin American leaders is this: Can our Pentecostal friends really teach us non-Pentecostals something? But even more basic is this question: Is the Spirit of God saying something to us non-Pentecostals as we take an objective look at our Pentecostal brothers and sisters in Latin America?

I can answer this question affirmatively, because I have begun to experience it in a significant way in my own life and ministry, as I explained in the

Introduction. The third wave of the power of the Holy Spirit in the 20th century is really a fulfillment of the dreams of the early Pentecostal leaders. When they began to experience the supernatural power of the Spirit in their everyday lives, they felt called to share this experience with believers in all existing denominations. They only started denominations when they were forced to do so by being totally rejected by their friends who were bound to tradition. But now an increasing number of churches which do not accept the label of either Pentecostal or charismatic are seeing New Testament signs and wonders manifested in their group through the ministry of their own insiders and they are excited about it.

I personally am seeing God's power for healing channeled through me in a way I never before dreamed possible. And as I mentally trace back my long pilgrimage to this point, I find that my contact with Latin American Pentecostals produced the beginning of the change. I share the experiences and lessons of this book with a prayer that God will do a similar thing in the lives of many others.

Notes

Chapter 1:
PENTECOSTAL GROWTH
IN LATIN AMERICA

1. Information for the section on Hoover was taken from his book *Historia del Avivamiento Pentecostal en Chile*.

2. John N. Vaughn, *The World's Twenty Largest Churches* (Grand Rapids: Baker, 1984), p. 210.

3. David B. Barrett, *World Christian Encyclopedia* (New York: Oxford University Press, 1982), p. 229.

4. Arno Enns, *Man, Milieu and Mission in Argentina* (Grand Rapids: Eerdmans, 1971), pp. 76-77.

5. Information for the section on Hicks came largely from a personal interview with him by the author at his Glendale, California, home, October 17, 1972, as well as from his book, *Millions Found Christ* (Los Angeles: Manifest Deliverance and Worldwide Evangelism Inc., 1956).

6. Hicks, p. 9.

7. Enns, *Man, Milieu...*, p. 206.

8. William R. Read, Victor M. Monterroso and Harmon A. Johnson, *Latin American Church Growth* (Grand Rapids: Eerdmans, 1969), p. 381.

9. Data on the Brazil section has been taken from Read, Monterroso and Johnson, *Latin American Church Growth*, as well as from a personal interview with Read, October 18, 1972.

10. John Thomas Nichol, *Pentecostalism* (New York: Harper & Row, 1966), pp. 132-133.

11. Emilio Conde, *Historia das Assembleias de Deus no Brasil* (Rio de Janeiro: Assembleias de Deus, 1960), pp. 25-26.

Chapter 2:
ENDUED WITH POWER
FROM ON HIGH

1. Willis C. Hoover, *Historia del Avivamiento Pentecostal en Chile (Valparaiso: Imprenta Excelsior, 1948), p. 31.*

2. *Alan Walker, "Where Pentecostalism Is Mushrooming," Christian Century* (January 17, 1968), p. 81.

3. John N. Vaughan, *The World's Twenty Largest Churches* (Grand Rapids: Baker, 1984), p. 222.

4. Caio Fabio D'Araujo Filho, *Nos Bastidores dos Espiritos* (Brazil: Belo Horizonte, 1982).

5. William R. Read, Victor M. Monterroso and Harmon A. Johnson, *Latin American Church Growth* (Grand Rapids: Eerdmans, 1969), p. 57.

6. Ralph Mahoney, "The Covering of Darkness," *World Map Digest* (March/April 1983), p. 2.

Chapter 3:
TAKING THE GOSPEL
TO THE PEOPLE

1. Information on the Foursquare in Guayaquil, Ecuador, was taken from Wayne Weld, *An Ecuadorian Impasse* (Chicago: Evangelical Covenant Church of America, 1968), and from a personal interview with Roberto Aguirre, June 8, 1972. Aguirre was the Foursquare missionary in charge of the crusade. He claims over 4,000 baptized members in 1966.

Chapter 4:
MOTHERS AND DAUGHTERS

1. The sources of information on the Foursquare Church in Ecuador are the same as indicated in note 1 for Chapter 3.

2. Donald C. Palmer, *Explosion of People Evangelism: An Analysis of Pentecostal Church Growth in Colombia* (Chicago: Moody Press, 1974), pp. 34-35.

3. Ibid., pp. 31-32.

4. Information on Brazil for Christ is taken from William R. Read, *New Patterns of Church Growth in Brazil* (Grand Rapids: Eerdmans, 1965), pp. 144-158; from Edward R. Murphy, *Brasil para Cristo* (Pasadena: Fuller Theological Seminary, unpublished research, 1972); and from a personal visit to the church and interview with Manoel de Melo in April 1983.

5. John N. Vaughan, *The World's Twenty Largest Churches* (Grand Rapids: Baker, 1984), p. 254.

6. William R. Read, Victor M. Monterroso and Harmon Johnson, *Latin American Church Growth* (Grand Rapids: Eerdmans, 1969), p. 68.

7. J. B. A. Kessler Jr., *A Study of the Older Protestant Missions and Churches in Peru and Chile* (Goes: Oosterbaan & le Cointer, 1967), p. 318.

8. Ignacio Vergara, *El Protestantismo en Chile* (Santiago: Editorial del Pacifico, 1962), p. 163.

9. Norbert E. Johnson, *The History, Dynamic and Problems of the Pentecostal Church in Chile* (Richmond: Union Theological Seminary, unpublished Th.M. thesis, 1970), p. 52.

10. David B. Barrett, ed., *World Christian Encyclopedia* (Oxford: Oxford University Press, 1982), p. 229.

11. Kessler, *A Study...*, p. 317.

Chapter 5:
SOWING THE SEED ON FERTILE SOIL

1. Emilio Willems, *Followers of the New Faith* (Nashville: Vanderbilt University Press, 1967), p. 248.

2. Christian Lalive, *Haven of the Masses* (London: Lutterworth Press, 1969), p. 224.

3. Donald A. McGavran, *Understanding Church Growth* (Grand Rapids: Eerdmans, 1980), pp. 295-313.

4. Lalive, *Haven...*, pp. 215-216.

5. Alan Walker, "Where Pentecostalism Is Mushrooming," *Christian Century* (January 17, 1968), p. 82.

6. William R. Read, Victor M. Monterroso and Harmon A. Johnson, *Latin American Church Growth* (Grand Rapids: Eerdmans, 1969), p. 356.

Chapter 6:
BODY LIFE BUILDS
HEALTHY CHURCHES

1. Ray Stedman, *Body Life* (Glendale: Regal Books, 1972).

2. Donald C. Palmer, *Explosion of People Evangelism: An Analysis of Pentecostal Church Growth in Colombia* (Chicago: Moody Press, 1974), p. 110.

3. Walter J. Hollenweger, *The Pentecostals* (Minneapolis: Augsburg Press, 1972), pp. 85, 88.

4. Donald A. McGavran, *Understanding Church Growth* (Grand Rapids: Eerdmans, 1980), p. 5.

5. Palmer, *Explosion...*, p. 130.

6. J. B. A. Kessler Jr., *A Study of the Older Pentecostal Missions and Churches in Peru and Chile* (Goes: Oosterbaan & le Cointre, 1967), p. 327.

7. John N. Vaughan, *The World's Twenty Largest Churches* (Grand Rapids: Baker, 1984), p. 214.

8. W. Philip Thornton, "The Cultural Key to Developing Strong Leaders," *Evangelical Missions Quarterly* (July 1984), p. 236.

9. Vaughan, *The World's Twenty...*, p. 249.

10. Christian Lalive, *Haven of the Masses* (London: Lutterworth Press, 1969), pp. 81, 83.

Chapter 7:
SEMINARIES IN THE STREETS

1. David C. Brackenridge, "Pentecostal Progress in Chile," *World Dominion* (September-October 1951), p. 296.

2. Christian Lalive, *Haven of the Masses* (London: Lutterworth Press, 1969), p. 70.

3. Donald A. McGavran, *Understanding Church Growth* (Grand Rapids: Eerdmans, 1980), pp. 295-313.

4. Lalive, *Haven...,* p. 72.

5. Melvin L. Hodges, *Growing Young Churches* (Chicago: Moody Press, 1970), p. 62.

Chapter 8:
IT'S FUN TO GO TO CHURCH

1. Emilio Castro, "Pentecostalism and Ecumenism in Latin America," *Christian Century* (September 27, 1972), p. 955.

2. J. B. A. Kessler Jr., *A Study of the Older Protestant Missions and Churches in Peru and Chile* (Goes: Oosterbaan & le Cointre, 1967), p. 323.

3. Howard A. Snyder, "The People of God—Implications for Church Structure," *Christianity Today* (October 27, 1972), p. 9.

4. Eugene Nida, "The Indigenous Churches in Latin America" (Buck Hill Falls: C.C.L.A., 1960), p. 10.

5. Donald C. Palmer, *Explosion of People Evangelism: An Analysis of Pentecostal Church Growth in Colombia* (Chicago: Moody Press, 1974), p. 123.

6. Ibid., p. 68.

7. Nida, *The Indigenous Churches...*, p. 8.

8. John N. Vaughan, *The World's Twenty Largest Churches* (Grand Rapids: Baker, 1984), p. 218.

Chapter 9:
PRAYING FOR THE SICK

1. Manuel Gaxiola, *La Serpiente y la Paloma* (South Pasadena: William Carey Library, 1970), p. 7.

2. This data was taken from notes on a personal interview with Roberto Aguirre, June 8, 1972.

3. Christian Lalive, *Haven of the Masses* (London: Lutterworth Press, 1969), pp. 197, 204.

4. This data comes from a personal interview with Ausencio Gonzalez, September 6, 1984.

5. William R. Read, Victor M. Monterroso and Harmon A. Johnson, *Latin American Church Growth* (Grand Rapids: Eerdmans, 1969), p. 323.

6. Lalive, *Haven...*, pp. 205-206.

7. Donald C. Palmer, *Explosion of People Evangelism: An Analysis of Pentecostal Church Growth in Colombia* (Chicago: Moody Press, 1974), p. 117.

8. Gaxiola, *La Serpiente...*, p. 10.

9. Palmer, *Explosion of People...*, p. 63.

10. Tommy Hicks, *Millions Found Christ* (Los Angeles: Manifest Deliverance and Worldwide Evangelism, Inc., 1956), pp. 21-23.

11. Edward Murphy, *Brazil Para Cristo* (Pasadena: Fuller Theological Seminary, 1972), pp. 16-20.

12. Harmon A. Johnson, *Authority Over the Spirits: Brazilian Spiritism and Evangelical Church Growth* (Pasadena: Fuller Theological Seminary, 1969, unpublished M.A. thesis).

13. Ibid., p. 91.

14. Ibid., pp. 102-103.

15. Ibid., p. 110.

Chapter 10:
IN NON-PENTECOSTAL CHURCHES

1. Ruben Lores, "Sobre Toda Carne" *Accion en Cristo para un Continente en Crisis* (Miami: Editorial Caribe, 1970), p. 11.

2. Information on the Colombian movement under Victor Landero was taken from David Howard, *Hammered as Gold* (New York: Harper & Row, 1969), and from a personal interview with Gregorio Landero, November 7, 1972.

3. Howard, *Hammered as Gold*, pp. 122-124.

4. Ibid., pp. 152-153.

5. See John Kenyon, "Gregorio Landero: He Helps Colombia's Forgotten People," *Latin America Evangelist* (November-December 1972).

6. J. B. A. Kessler Jr., *A Study of the Older Protestant Missions and Churches in Peru and Chile* (Goes: Oosterbaan & le Cointre, 1967), p. 127.

7. Lores, "Sobre Toda Carne," p. 13.

8. Howard, *Hammered as Gold*, p. 146.

9. Information on the renewal in San Jose, Costa Rica, was taken from notes on a message by Victor Monterroso in September 1972; from information supplied by A. William Cook Jr. and Ruben Lores; and from personal knowledge of the situation.

10. A. William Cook Jr., typescript of research paper presented to the faculty of the Latin American Biblical Seminary, San Jose, Costa Rica, n.d., p. 16.

Index

Index